The territorial Conservative Party

New Perspectives on the Right

Series editor
Richard Hayton

The study of conservative politics, broadly defined, is of enduring scholarly interest and importance, and is also of great significance beyond the academy. In spite of this, for a variety of reasons the study of conservatism and conservative politics was traditionally regarded as something of a poor relation in comparison to the intellectual interest in 'the Left'. In the British context this changed with the emergence of Thatcherism, which prompted a greater critical focus on the Conservative Party and its ideology, and a revitalisation of Conservative historiography. *New Perspectives on the Right* aims to build on this legacy by establishing a series identity for work in this field. It will publish the best and most innovative titles drawn from the fields of sociology, history, cultural studies and political science and hopes to stimulate debate and interest across disciplinary boundaries. *New Perspectives* is not limited in its historical coverage or geographical scope, but is united by its concern to critically interrogate and better understand the history, development, intellectual basis and impact of the Right. Nor is the series restricted by its methodological approach: it will encourage original research from a plurality of perspectives. Consequently, the series will act as a voice and forum for work by scholars engaging with the politics of the right in new and imaginative ways.

Reconstructing conservatism? The Conservative party in opposition, 1997–2010
Richard Hayton

Conservative orators from Baldwin to Cameron
Edited by Richard Hayton and Andrew S. Crines

The right and the recession
Edward Ashbee

The territorial Conservative Party

Devolution and party change in Scotland and Wales

Alan Convery

Manchester University Press

Copyright © Alan Convery 2016

The right of Alan Convery to be identified as the author of this work has been asserted by him in accordance with the Copyright, Designs and Patents Act 1988.

Published by Manchester University Press
Altrincham Street, Manchester M1 7JA
www.manchesteruniversitypress.co.uk

British Library Cataloguing-in-Publication Data
A catalogue record for this book is available from the British Library

Library of Congress Cataloging-in-Publication Data applied for

ISBN 978 1 7849 9131 9 hardback

First published 2016

The publisher has no responsibility for the persistence or accuracy of URLs for any external or third-party internet websites referred to in this book, and does not guarantee that any content on such websites is, or will remain, accurate or appropriate.

Typeset by Out of House Publishing
Printed in Great Britain
by CPI Group (UK) Ltd, Croydon CR0 4YY

Contents

List of tables	*page* vi
Acknowledgements	vii
Introduction	1
Part I Theory and context	**9**
1 When and why do political parties change?	11
2 The UK Conservative Party: statewide context	20
Part II Scotland and Wales	**33**
3 Devolution, party change and the Scottish Conservative Party	35
4 Devolution, party change and the Welsh Conservative Party	75
5 Comparing party change in Scotland and Wales	106
Part III Conclusion	**117**
Devolution, party politics and conservatism	119
References	129
Index	141

Tables

1.1	Conservative Party electoral performance in Scotland and Wales, 1999–2011	*page* 2
2.1	Conservative Party performance at UK general elections, 1979–2010	23
2.2	Detterbeck and Hepburn's (2010: 116) typology of statewide party strategies	24
2.3	Conservative shadow secretaries of state for Scotland, 1997–2010	25
2.4	Conservative shadow secretaries of state for Wales, 1997–2010	25
2.5	Leaders of the UK Conservative Party, 1997–	26
3.1	Conservative electoral performance in Scotland at Westminster elections	37
3.2	Leaders of the Scottish Conservative Party, 1999–2013	47
3.3	Scottish Conservative performance at Scottish Parliament elections	52
3.4	Organisational structure recommended by the Strathclyde Commission (1998)	57
3.5	Conservative Members of the Scottish Parliament, 1999–2011	64
3.6	The evolution of Scottish Conservative policy on key public services	71
4.1	Conservative electoral performance in Wales at Westminster elections	78
4.2	Welsh Assembly Governments since 1999	81
4.3	Welsh Conservative performance at National Assembly elections	86
4.4	Structure of the Welsh Conservative Party	89
4.5	Conservative Members of the Welsh Assembly, 1999–2011	94
5.1	Indicators of autonomy for the Welsh and Scottish Conservatives	110
5.2	Conservative Party change in Scotland and Wales, 1997–2011	115

Acknowledgements

The origins of this book lie in doctoral research that I undertook at the University of Strathclyde between 2010 and 2013. This was made possible by the award of a university scholarship, for which I am most grateful. I would like to thank my supervisor, James Mitchell, for guiding this project from the beginning and for the many excellent conversations about Scottish politics. Thomas Lundberg has been my 'unofficial' supervisor and mentor since first encouraging me to pursue an academic career when I attended his Scottish Politics Honours class. I have greatly appreciated his advice and encouragement. I first presented parts of this analysis to members of the Political Studies Association's Conservatives and Conservatism specialist group. I would like to thank them, especially Richard Hayton and Matt Beech, for being a patient and supportive audience.

Douglas Pattullo's encouragement and encyclopaedic knowledge of the Scottish Conservatives have been invaluable. Further afield, thank you to Adam Evans at Cardiff University for keeping me right about the intricacies of Welsh politics. Many serving and former politicians and officials gave freely of their time and expertise to talk to me about the Conservative Party. I would like to thank them for their generosity and I hope I have managed to capture something of their experience. Tony Mason at Manchester University Press and two anonymous reviewers have also been especially helpful.

I could not have reached this point without the support of my parents, Isobel and Bill Convery. This book is dedicated to them. Finally, thank you to James for all of his love and support.

Alan Convery
Edinburgh, September 2015

Introduction

> If you think back, we were seen as doing very well under devolution, as opposed to the Welsh, who were seen to be backward and the Welsh party is now of course ... everyone [says]: 'Oh, look at the Welsh model, that's what you need to learn from.'
> (Interview with Scottish official 4, 30 November 2012)

All organisations have to adapt to changing circumstances. In the business world, this might be associated with the arrival of new technology or the changing habits of customers. In a similar way, political parties that want to be successful have to respond to changes in society and the policy environment. However, like some businesses, political parties often fail to adapt or decide to pursue what in hindsight turns out to be the wrong strategy. They may continue to flog spools in the era of the digital camera. There is therefore a complicated set of interactions between the perception of the need to adapt and the comfort that may be found in maintaining the familiar status quo. A central question in the study of political parties is how (and how far) they change in response to their environment.

This book is concerned with how this question has played out in two political parties that had to adapt to substantial changes after 1997: the Scottish and Welsh Conservative parties. Reflecting on her 1979 speech to the Scottish Conservative Party conference, Margaret Thatcher remarked that, 'Life is not easy for Scottish Tories; nor was it to become easier' (Thatcher, 1993: 35). The Conservative Governments (1979–1997) were a particularly difficult time for the territorial Conservative Party. In Scotland and Wales, the party suffered a crisis of both popularity and legitimacy that led to the return of not a single Conservative MP outside England at the 1997 general election. The party then suffered the additional trauma of dealing with the implementation of the devolved territorial governments that it had long campaigned against, and which seemed inimical to its conception of unionism. The sub-state Welsh and Scottish branches of the statewide UK Conservative Party both embarked on post-devolution life with a difficult inheritance.

However, the puzzle at the heart of this book concerns their seemingly contrasting fortunes since then. While the Welsh Conservatives appear to have staged a recovery since 1997, the Scottish Conservatives have been much less successful. It has also become accepted wisdom in the Scottish Conservative Party that it has

Table 1.1 Conservative Party electoral performance in Scotland and Wales, 1999–2011

Election	Members of the Scottish Parliament	Members of the Welsh Assembly
1999	18	9
2003	18	11
2007	17	12
2011	15	14

Source: Rallings and Thrasher (2009); National Assembly for Wales (2011); Scottish Parliament (2013).

lessons to learn from its Welsh colleagues. This book seeks to analyse how both parties have adapted to devolution and the reasons why one party may have changed more substantially or in different ways than the other.

The central research question of this book is to ask how the Welsh and Scottish Conservative parties adapted to devolution. In answering this question, I draw on the tools of comparative political science and the existing work on political parties and adaptation. I try to show how the territorial Conservative Party fits into wider debates about the nature of party change and the challenges faced by statewide parties in regional contexts.

Multi-level party politics and statewide parties

A statewide party is a party that competes in elections simultaneously at the central or national level also and across more than one sub-state level. Such a definition would include the UK Labour Party, which competes at Westminster and in Scotland and Wales. However, it would exclude, for instance, the Scottish National Party, which has a presence at both the Scottish Parliament and Westminster, but which does not compete in Wales or Northern Ireland. Statewide parties may thus be distinguished from stateless nationalist or regionalist parties (SNRPs), such as Plaid Cymru in Wales (Hepburn, 2009 Fabre and Swenden, 2013: 343). The Scottish and Welsh Conservative parties are sub-state branches of the statewide UK Conservative Party. It is an archetypal statewide party as it competes in Scotland and Wales, at UK elections, and at a supranational level in the European Parliament.

The sub-state branches of statewide parties face a series of difficult choices in deciding the extent to which they should adapt to multi-level politics. How much should their policies differ from the statewide party? Should they give up influence at the centre for more local autonomy (Van Biezen and Hopkin, 2006; Detterbeck and Hepburn, 2010; Alonso, 2012)? They must also find a coherent way be both defenders of the constitutional status quo and champions for regional distinctiveness. These tensions are reflected in decisions about the parties' constitutional structures as well as their policy platform and financial arrangements (Hopkin, 2009; Thorlakson, 2009). Statewide parties must find a balance between emphasising the regional and the national (Roller and Van Houten, 2003).

There are five central reasons why it is important for political scientists to study the behaviour of statewide parties and their sub-state branches (Fabre and Swenden, 2013: 343). First, the trend in most OECD countries over the past 30 years has been one of decentralisation towards sub-state levels of government (Hooghe *et al.*, 2010). While the twentieth century overall may have displayed a trend towards the nationalisation of politics (Caramani, 2004; Chhibber and Kollman, 2004), there is now increasing evidence of decentralisation in the nature of party competition in Western Europe (Hough and Jeffery, 2003, 2006; Johns *et al.*, 2013). In Scotland, for instance, party competition was always different from the UK level and is becoming more so (Miller, 1981; Bohrer and Krutz, 2005). Parties increasingly operate as multi-level organisations that compete in elections with different dynamics and perhaps different party systems in several parts of a state. The study of only a party's 'core' level (Deschouwer, 2003) gives an incomplete picture of its activities, especially when it may face the challenge of competing against regionalist parties at a sub-state level (Meguid, 2010; Toubeau, 2011).

Second, as Fabre and Swenden (2013: 343) argue, 'By shifting the unit of analysis to the region (or the local level), the comparative method can be meaningfully applied to regional party systems and party organizations within the same state.' This allows us to compare strategies for territorial management across parties and different sub-state regions, and across time.

Third, statewide parties perform an important function in linking not only citizens to government, but also policies and governments at the different levels of a state (Filippov *et al.*, 2004; Bolleyer, 2011; Fabre and Swenden, 2013: 343). Statewide parties contribute to the ties that keep a multi-level state together. They also provide the structures through which statewide party leaders attempt to influence sub-state politics and policy. When the same party is in power at a national and sub-state level, statewide parties can also smooth policy coordination or intergovernmental dispute resolution (McEwen *et al.*, 2012). The fact that they are closer to citizens may also help the sub-state branches of statewide parties do a better job of linking citizens to national political decisions (Fabre and Swenden, 2013: 350).

Fourth, statewide parties provide central party politicians and central government with a measure of legitimacy when they take decisions at a national level that have an impact on sub-state regions. Even if a statewide party performs poorly in sub-state elections, the fact of it standing candidates in every area of the country lends it a degree of legitimacy. The structures of the statewide Conservative Party in Scotland also provided, for instance, the forum through which senior national Conservative politicians, such as the prime minister, engaged in the debate on Scottish independence.

Finally, and of central importance to this study, parties operating simultaneously at different levels provide interesting cases through which to explore the nature of party change. Comparisons between parties at the national centre and at the sub-state level also allow us to explore the extent to which national party change affects sub-state parties and vice versa.

Devolution in the United Kingdom

The plurinational nature of the UK's 'state of unions' (Mitchell, 2010) and the strengthening of administrative devolution, particularly in the post-war period, have resulted in UK political parties that to some extent always operated as multi-level organisations. However, the 1997–2001 Labour Government's programme of devolution made the multi-level nature of the political system much more explicit and more urgent. For Bogdanor (2001: 1), devolution is the most significant constitutional reform in the UK since the Great Reform Act in the nineteenth century.

It required all of the UK's statewide parties to reconsider their territorial organisation (Fabre, 2008; Bratberg, 2009). They were forced to negotiate a response to a much more explicit 'regional/national dilemma' (Roller and Van Houten, 2003). Moreover, in the UK, this strategic decision was compounded by the nature of devolution itself. The devolution reforms of 1998 posed as many, if not more, questions as answers (Jeffery, 2007). First, devolution in the UK is quite radically asymmetrical. Not only have different levels of autonomy been granted to Scotland, Wales and Northern Ireland, there has also been no devolution to the regions of England. For Flinders and Curry (2008), this has resulted in a form of 'bi-constitutionality' in which the traditional Westminster rules of the game continue to apply to UK-level elections and government, alongside more consensual approaches in the devolved UK regions. The devolution reforms were explicitly designed not to interfere with the UK centre's ability to take decisions about the governance of England or the UK (Mitchell, 2010; Convery, 2014a).

Second, in this context, the devolution arrangements did not create a federal system of government. Tony Blair in particular was ambivalent about the nature of the reforms he was implementing (see, for example, Ashdown, 2001: 446) and the preservation of the doctrine of parliamentary sovereignty lies at the heart of both the Scotland and Wales Acts (1998). However, for Vernon Bogdanor (2009) the effect of devolution has been to create a de facto quasi-federal UK. Thus, whilst it is theoretically possible that the Westminster Parliament could still abolish the Scottish Parliament and Welsh Assembly, it is almost impossible to imagine the circumstances under which it would do so. Such a decision would likely result in a constitutional crisis that could lead to Scotland leaving the Union. Moreover, the British Government has made it clear that it accepts the sovereignty of the Scottish people on the matter of secession. It recognises Scotland's unilateral right to secede. Compared to other federalised or decentralised states, this is a highly unusual feature of the UK (Melding, 2013: 11–12). As King (2007: 179) argues: 'With the coming of devolution to Scotland and Wales [the] single locus of sovereign authority no longer exists. Or, if it does exist, it exists only on paper.'

However, whilst the devolved legislatures (particularly the Scottish Parliament) have substantial *self-rule* powers, the extent of *shared rule* – sub-state government input into national decisions – is extremely limited in the UK (Swenden, 2010). They are allowed considerable freedom on the areas devolved to them, but there are few formal mechanisms for them to influence UK Government policy. Thus, the UK Government attaches no strings to the block grants it gives to the devolved governments. They may spend their money exactly as they choose. Crucially, they are also free to organise their public services in a manner that pleases them. This has led to substantial divergence from policies in England, particularly in the areas of health and education.

Statewide political parties in the UK must, therefore, negotiate the uneven structures of devolution. In particular, for Hazell (2006: 1), England is 'the gaping hole in the devolution settlement'. For parties whose core level is at the UK and who draw most of their MPs from England, this creates a tricky backdrop for territorial politics. In Jim Bulpitt's (1982: 144) words, 'for the Conservative Party the United Kingdom is, and always has been, a particularly difficult piece of political real estate to manage'.

The Scottish and Welsh Conservative parties

In this context, the Welsh and Scottish Conservative parties present an interesting case for comparison. Of all the UK statewide parties, the Conservatives had the furthest to travel in terms of accepting the new devolved institutions. Whilst the party had become adept at deepening and entrenching administrative devolution (Mitchell, 2003), it set its face since the early 1980s firmly against moving any further. All of the other statewide parties, alongside the Scottish National Party and Plaid Cymru, supported devolution. In 1998, therefore, both the Welsh and Scottish Conservative parties had to carry out an abrupt change in attitude if they were to participate in the new devolved institutions.

Both parties were also haunted by similar ghosts of the past. The legacy (economic, political and mythological) of the Thatcher Governments (1979–1990) and her perceived mishandling of territorial politics cast a shadow over Conservatives in Wales and Scotland. Well into the third term of the Scottish Parliament, Members of the Scottish Parliament (MSPs) were still invoking the memory of the Thatcher Governments to warn about the dangers of Conservative policies (Torrance, 2009: 254). The rapid economic changes of the 1980s and 1990s also had a disproportionate impact on Scotland and Wales due in part to the large concentrations of heavy industry (Stewart, 2009).

Thus, whilst it is a gross exaggeration to suggest that the Welsh and Scottish Conservatives both faced the same challenges in 1997, it would be fair to say that they started post-devolution life with a broadly similar inheritance: no MPs, a difficult past and new institutions that they had stridently campaigned against. Having both set out with a comparably poor hand to play, their contrasting fortunes since then present an interesting case study to examine how and why they might have responded to different pressures to change. Scotland and Wales might both be considered 'cold climates' for Conservatives (Kendrick and McCrone, 1989; Torrance, 2009).

Comparing party change

In order to compare the Scottish and Welsh Conservative parties, this study uses an analytical framework derived from the literature on party change and the literature on multi-level party politics. I compare the Scottish and Welsh Conservative parties using a series of drivers and manifestations of change. This book is therefore a qualitative case study. It seeks to understand the processes of change and continuity in the Welsh and Scottish Conservative parties in the post-devolution period. The central question is: how did the Welsh and Scottish Conservative parties adapt to devolution and multi-level politics? Answering such a question requires an in-depth focus on the post-devolution political environment and, most especially, on the people, organisations and ideas that had the potential to drive party change. Only in this way will we be able to isolate and examine the complex social processes that affected these two parties.

We are therefore explicitly concerned with the history of the post-1997 Scottish and Welsh Conservative parties. History matters here for three central reasons (Steinmo, 2008: 127). First, acquiring expertise in certain cases is an essential task for political scientists (Kavanagh, 1991; Gerring, 2001: 122; Tilly, 2006; Burnham et al., 2008: 174). As Tilly (2006: 420) describes, 'Not only do all political processes occur in history and therefore call for knowledge of their historical contexts, but also where and when processes occur influence *how* they occur. History thus becomes an essential element of sound explanations for political processes.'

Second, as Steinmo (2008: 127) explains, 'behaviour, attitudes and strategic choices take place inside particular social, political, economic and even cultural contexts'. Actors are shaped by their surroundings in ways that cannot be explained fully if they are taken out of their temporal setting and treated simply as variables. We cannot hope to fully understand a party's behaviour by simply studying the raw output of election results or counting how many times words appear in manifestos. Although political parties in general have much in common, often their actions can only be explained through detailed knowledge of history, idiosyncrasies and people. Their specificities should not be viewed as a barrier to parsimonious theory building or as a difficult variable to codify and aggregate: they are instead a reflection of complex social realities (Flyvbjerg, 2001: 86; Della Porta, 2008: 207). A case study reaches the heart of these questions.

Finally, actors' perceptions and expectations are themselves shaped by the past (Steinmo, 2008: 128). Political actors are students of political history whose ideas and attitudes are products of their own past experiences and their own interpretations of events. The attitudes in government of Margaret Thatcher and Geoffrey Howe, for instance, were indelibly marked by their experience in Edward Heath's cabinet; John Major's feelings about inflation were influenced by his own personal circumstances; public policy-making in post-devolution Scotland is informed by an interpretation of the Conservative Governments (1979–1997). This book is, therefore, also explicitly interested in the meaning that actors attach to their actions. What to a political scientist may seem like a 'rational' course to follow may be ignored in a political party not only because change is difficult, but also because party elites interpret events and problems differently.

These assumptions about the nature of the research question may be summarised as a historical institutionalist approach. Steinmo (2008: 126) describes this approach as standing between a rational choice institutionalism (which emphasises how rules shape an individual's choices and interpretations of how to maximise personal gain) and sociological institutionalism (which emphasises how human beings naturally follow social norms in pursuing their goals). Instead, it views humans as '*both* norm-abiding rule followers *and* self-interested rational actors. How one behaves depends on the individual, on the context and on the rules' (Steinmo, 2008: 126).

Outline

The analysis proceeds in three main stages: theory and context; detailed analysis of the Scottish and Welsh cases; and conclusions. Chapter 1 discusses what we know about party change and multi-level politics. It sets out an analytical framework based on a series of drivers and manifestations of change. Chapter 2 then discusses the main changes that occurred at the top of the Conservative Party after devolution. It sets out the statewide context for decisions made at the sub-state level and suggests key developments that may have affected the thinking or environment of the party beyond the centre.

The main analysis begins with consideration of the Scottish case in Chapter 3. This study finds that, until 2014, the main levers of party change were in the hands of elected politicians who chose not to use them. Beyond party organisation, devolution was not a driver of change. Instead, interpretations of electoral performance mattered more than changes in leadership or dominant faction. The 2014 independence referendum forced the party to come to terms with devolution through its own proposals for further powers, but this policy change has yet to extend to any other area. However, in the Welsh case (Chapter 4), significant party change was much more in evidence. In particular, an early change of leadership was a key driver of changes in strategy and policy (although the issue of further devolution always remained thorny). There were no organisational changes after the initial creation of a more distinct Welsh Conservative Party after devolution, but the party leadership pushed at the limits of their small measure of autonomy.

Comparing the two cases (Chapter 5) reveals that people mattered more than party structures when explaining party change in these two parties. Fundamentally, both parties interpreted their problems differently. On paper, both parties had different levels of autonomy, but in practice party constitutions mattered little here. The enacted party organisation gave the Welsh Conservatives considerable room to innovate and their comparative lack of institutionalisation became an advantage. Finally, we draw the two cases together and consider how they fit into a wider understanding of party change and multi-level politics. What does it mean to be a statewide party in the UK post-devolution and, in particular, post-referendum?

PART I

Theory and context

1

When and why do political parties change?

This chapter sets out an analytical framework to compare the Scottish and Welsh Conservative parties. They are two branches of a statewide political party that confront the challenges of dealing with multi-level politics. This chapter considers what we know about change in political parties and places a particular emphasis on the factors that affect parties at the sub-state level. Taking Harmel and Janda's (1994) model of national party change as its starting point, it outlines a framework to analyse sub-state party change. Two broad sections cover the drivers (why?) of party change and the manifestations (how?) of party change.

However, whilst isolating these different factors provides a common framework for analysis, we must be conscious of the fact that explanations for party change cannot be so neatly packaged. Party change (or stasis) in the real world is the result of a complicated series of interactions among institutions, ideas and people. In particular, a split between drivers and manifestations is inherently artificial. Party change cannot be easily broken down into dependent and independent variables. Changes in personnel, for instance, could be considered as both a driver and a manifestation of party change. Therefore, having used these headings to draw out and compare similar processes in both parties, I come back in Chapter 5 to draw the analysis together.

What drives party change?

In complex organisations like political parties, defining and measuring change is difficult (Mair, 1989). It involves an element of subjectivity, both in terms of what constitutes change in the first place, and perhaps more so in evaluating how significant that change is. For some parties, involving party membership in a leadership election could be a banal and evolutionary development; for others, it might represent something of a revolution. Moreover, party elites themselves may perceive changes to be more significant than they appear to an outside observer, particularly if they have been involved in implementing them.

Harmel and Janda (1994) provide a systematic framework for analysing party change and this has been applied to several case studies. However, like much parties research and theorising it deals only with change at the national level (Deschouwer,

2005; Fabre and Swenden, 2013; Jeffery and Schakel, 2013). In order to address the research questions of this study, it is adapted and refined to make it sensitive to the concerns of parties like the Scottish and Welsh Conservatives that operate at the sub-state level but nevertheless retain a link to the statewide party system.

Therefore, we will discuss in turn several possible causes of party change: change in party leadership; change in a party's dominant faction; the external shock of electoral defeat; the effects of electoral competition at the sub-state level; and changes in public opinion. Crucially, this study agrees with Harmel and Janda (1994: 262) that party changes do not 'just happen'. Clearly, changes in a party's environment may *encourage* party change. However, these do not in themselves passively cause parties to change. Instead, changes in a party's environment must be consciously absorbed by party elites in order to bring about change in political parties. Parties may choose not to change at all in response to changes in the society or institutions in which they operate. It is possible for parties to react in entirely different ways to the same environmental changes. They need not all follow strictly functional pressures (Fabre, 2008; Bratberg, 2009; Swenden and Maddens, 2009).

Thus, for Deschouwer (1992: 17), ' "perception" is the intermediate variable that has to be placed between objective facts and the reactions of the parties'. Similarly, for Wilson (1994: 264), 'parties are not simply passive recipients of pressures from their socioeconomic, cultural, institutional and competitive environment'. It is therefore also the case that parties might change as a result of internal shifts that are unrelated to their outside environment (Panebianco, 1988: 241–242).

Leadership change

The Scottish and Welsh Conservative parties have each had three different post-devolution leaders. However, the evidence on the impact of leadership change on party change is mixed. Harmel *et al.* (1995: 6) hypothesise that: 'Leadership change is associated with party change, even with all possible direct effects of poor electoral performance (and resulting leadership changes) already removed.' Thus it is 'a sufficient, though not necessary, condition for party change'. Leaders are central interpreters of the reasons for poor election results and are often the instigators of organisational or programmatic reform. Their assessment of whether reform is necessary and their attempts to block it may have a significant impact on the scope for change. As Wilson (1994: 264) points out: 'party leaders and reformers as the key intervening variable that determines whether or not parties will, in fact, respond to any of these factors that make transformation possible or desirable'. Moreover, as Harmel *et al.* (1995: 4) note: 'Different leaders will assess things differently; different leaders have different abilities with which to develop and implement changes when they do want them.' Leaders with an electoral mandate for change from the party membership may be in an especially powerful position to drive through party change.

However, the impact of leadership change on party change will be affected by the structure and culture of different political parties. For instance, in the highly centralised and office-seeking UK Conservative Party, a high degree of autonomy is given to the party leadership. A new leader therefore has considerable scope to radically alter strategy and policy positions without the express permission of party members or officials (Bale, 2010: 17). During the coalition negotiations in 2010, William Hague observed that the Conservative Party 'is an absolute monarchy but this is qualified by regicide' (quoted in Laws, 2010: 102).

Leadership change in a party that prizes internal democracy may not have as much impact. Thus, Harmel *et al.* (1995: 7) hypothesise that: 'The relationship between leadership changes and party change is stronger for parties with strong leadership structures than for parties with severely limited leaders.' In contrast, in parties where the membership exercise strong oversight and control over the party leadership, it might be expected that change is less likely because the leadership has to a much greater extent to ensure they take the party members with them (Samuels, 2004: 1020).

Harmel *et al.*'s (1995: 12–14) cross-national data of six parties for the period 1950–1990 largely supports both hypotheses. Party change usually follows leadership change and this effect is most pronounced in parties (like the German CDU and the British Conservative Party) that have strong leadership structures. The effect is smaller in more decentralised parties like the German SPD and the British Labour Party. More recently, Schumacher *et al.* (2013) find that parties that are controlled mainly by the leadership tend to respond to changes in the mean voter's position, whereas parties with much more internal democracy tend to follow their own voters. Meyer's (2013: 154) study of policy shifts in parties in ten European countries concludes that 'although voters are more likely to accept party policy shifts of newly elected leaders, leadership changes do not lead to larger party policy shifts'.

More in-depth case studies have generated further mixed evidence about the impact of party leadership changes. Müller (1997) finds that changes in leadership were the driving force behind changes in the Austrian Socialist Party's campaigning techniques. Indeed, alongside electoral defeats and changes in dominant factions, 'leadership change must be considered as the single most important factor' (Müller, 1997: 309). However, Bille (1997) finds that in the Danish Social Democratic Party, changes of leadership tended to facilitate programmatic changes already in motion, rather than be the drivers of those changes themselves. It may also be that changes in leadership have much more slow-burning consequences for political parties. In the rather unwieldy structures of the German CDU, Clemens (2009) finds that the impact of Angela Merkel's leadership was a long process, rather than a single event.

In multi-level parties like the UK Conservative Party, it is likely that there will be tensions between the national and regional party leaderships, particularly over issues like autonomy and candidate selection (Hopkin, 2003). Where leaderships at both levels are in agreement about organisational or programmatic change, then this change is more likely. Where there is significant disagreement (if, for instance, leaders at different levels come from different party factions), then the resulting arguments may make party change more difficult.

The effect of leadership change on party change is therefore mixed (Fagerholm, 2015: 3), but we may tentatively say that party leaders are in a strong position to drive change when they have the institutional resources to do so (in terms of a mandate, a culture of hierarchy or a perceived legitimacy) or if they move with the grain of the party membership who share an analysis of the problems that need to be solved (Panebianco, 1988: 246). Both Meyer (2013: 204) and Schumacher *et al.* (2013) find that party leaders with strong organisations can more easily change their policy platform. However, party change may not follow leadership change simply because the leaders who take over do not believe it is required or because they are simply not dominant enough to impose it (see, for instance, Fell, 2009).

Change in dominant faction: factions at both levels

Parties are coalitions of interests and factions. As Katz and Mair (1993: 6) emphasise:

> *a party itself is a political system.* Within each of the three faces of party organization [voluntary, governing and bureaucratic], politics is endlessly played out, with different coalitions of forces and actors striving for dominance. Politics is clearly part of the interactions of all three faces, reflecting the tensions that underlie their various interrelationships, as well as the struggle for relative influence within the organization *tout court.*

Such factional tensions are played out, for instance, in the UK Labour Party in the split between Blairite and Brownite groups, and in the Liberal Democrats between 'Orange Book' liberals and more left-wing social democrats. If there is such strong disagreement between factions about the future direction of a political party, then the replacement in leadership positions or dominance of one faction over another could be expected to make party change more likely (Harmel and Janda, 1994: 267). Panebianco (1988: 244) also argues that party change is correlated with shifts in internal power dynamics that are often subsequently entrenched in changes to party rules.

In their analysis of five parties in the UK and Germany in the period 1950–1990, Harmel and Tan (2003) find that party change does tend to follow changes in a party's dominant faction. However, based on their mixed findings, they conclude that in situations where a new dominant faction's position is less secure (due, for instance, to lukewarm support in the party membership or bureaucracy), then new leaders from that dominant faction may be instrumental in driving change (Harmel and Tan, 2003: 422).

However, we also need to consider the possibilities of intra-party factionalism that straddles the different levels of a party. In a federal or decentralised state, there exists the possibility for different factions to control different branches of a party. There is also the potential for alliances among factions with similar beliefs operating at different levels of a party. As Verge and Gómez (2011: 3) point out, 'factional conflict is potentially aggravated by territorial conflict between party levels'. The dominant faction's reaction to a challenge is conditioned both by the extent of devolution within the party and the nature of the strategy used by the insurgent faction. Organisational change is therefore prompted not only by a dominant faction's vision of the future of a party, but also because it is a tool to control factions.

Electoral defeat

A particularly emphatic electoral defeat is likely to concentrate minds in any political party, particularly if that party tends towards seeking office or votes. However, the impact of such defeats depends not only on how they affect a party's sense of its own purpose, but also, crucially, how they are *perceived* by party members and elites. The party leadership is thus, once again, one of the central interpreters of events and their significance (Deschouwer, 1992: 17; Wilson, 1994: 281). In her study of parties' policy changes over time in 23 countries Somer-Topcu (2009) found that higher levels of votes lost tended to result in more significant policy changes.

It is therefore useful in this context to consider different types of electoral defeat. Janda *et al.* (1995: 182–183) propose a five-fold typology. A *calamitous* election is interpreted as a decisive rejection of a party or its policy stance or the clear endorsement of an electoral rival; a *disappointing* election will hurt but may result in a smaller loss of seats or the winning of fewer seats than the party expected; a *tolerable* election is accepted as the ordinary rough and tumble of politics with perhaps a small loss or gain in votes and seats; a *gratifying* election is one which can be interpreted as a vote of confidence in a party's performance or policies, accompanied perhaps by a gain in seats (beyond what was expected), allowing the party to enter government; and, finally, a *triumphal* election involves a big gain in seats and votes or the decisive defeat of a rival (Janda *et al.*, 1995: 182–183).

Electoral competition

The nature of electoral competition at the sub-state level may be a crucial driver of party change (Meguid, 2005, 2008). The regional branches of statewide parties face a particular challenge in appearing credible at both the national and sub-state level. In particular, statewide parties may face electoral threats from SNRPs who operate solely at the sub-state level. These are political parties 'whose core business is sub-state territorial empowerment, whereby empowerment involves seeking to represent and advance the particular interests of the stateless territory and where territorial interests may be economic, political, social, cultural or symbolic in nature' (Hepburn, 2009: 482). Thus, we will pay special attention to electoral competition in the Scottish and Welsh contexts from the Scottish National Party and Plaid Cymru. As Elias (2011: 8) argues, 'a statewide party that dismisses the territorial issues raised by its autonomist competitors when this is something that is important to voters is likely to be punished due to the perception that it is out of touch with political reality'.

Public opinion

It is important to recognise the difficulties parties face in deciding how to react to public opinion (at a national or regional level) in order to strengthen their position. As Budge (1994: 445) points out, even opinion polls are not necessarily reliable indicators of how policy affects votes:

> They may in general terms identify certain issues as important to electors, but leave it open as to whether these will necessarily affect their vote. For example, an overwhelming majority of British electors in the 1980s and 1990s placed welfare among their top priorities, at the same time as a plurality voted for a tax-cutting Conservative government whose attitudes were hostile to welfare.

Faced with these uncertainties, parties use their ideology as a guide for approaching issues of policies and strategy. Budge (1994) concludes that while parties' policies may shift, their core ideological beliefs remain fairly stable over time. Adams *et al.* (2004) also find that past election results have little systematic effect on a party's ideology. Instead they find that parties tend only to shift their policy positions when public opinion moves substantially in the opposite direction. Thus parties on the left will shift in a rightward direction only when public opinion moderates significantly (Adams *et al.*, 2004: 590). Parties also react to the movements of other parties in a system. Adams and Somer-Topcu (2009) find that parties tend to shift their policies in the same direction as their opponents in the last election. Parties are also particularly sensitive to shifts in other parties of the same ideological family. There is also some evidence that centre-right parties are more sensitive to shifts in public opinion than social democratic parties (Adams *et al.*, 2009: 625–626). However, overall, any attempt to change a party's policy programme is likely to encounter resistance.

How do parties change?

Having been affected by some of the above drivers, parties must then decide the extent to which they will reform themselves to adapt to new circumstances. In this study we are interested in change in the sub-state branches of statewide parties. For these parties, a change in the territorial structure of a state poses especially difficult problems. How can they reconcile their support for the central state with their need to be seen to stand up for regional interests? Again, in order to isolate and examine individual processes here, I separate the manifestations of party change into three broad areas: changes in organisation, personnel and policy. The literature on party policy change is the most extensive, but the other areas are also crucial to understanding the adaptation of statewide parties in the UK. In particular, party organisation (and the extent of sub-state party autonomy) is a critical area for examination here.

Toubeau and Massetti (2013: 302) suggest that statewide parties faced with decentralisation can adapt according to three central logics of action. First, parties might follow an electoral strategy and base their adaptation on doing whatever it takes to maximise their vote share. Second, if an ideological logic prevails, then considerations of electoral politics will be secondary to the desire to stick to a certain idea of how the state should be organised (perhaps regardless of the consequences at elections). Finally, parties might adapt according to a territorial logic: they concentrate on securing particular benefits for their region, perhaps involving pushing for changes in the terms of membership of the central state.

Organisation and sub-state organisational autonomy

Party organisation is an important expression of a party's attitude and strategy towards its regional branches. It is also a key lever of party change. Parties that have just suffered electoral defeats often respond by engaging in organisational change (see, for instance: Kelly, 2003; Fell, 2009; Bale, 2010: 74; Scottish Labour Party, 2011). However, as Ball (2005: 12–13) points out in relation to the Conservative Party, 'activity here can be a substitute for tackling more fundamental and difficult problems in other areas'.

Statewide parties face a series of difficult choices in deciding how to organise themselves at the sub-state level. We may group these into four broad categories: candidate selection, leadership selection, finance and policy-making (Laffin et al., 2007: 90–92). First, how much autonomy does the statewide party allow its branches in terms of candidate selection? This may range from a completely decentralised process in which sub-state parties control all aspects of selecting candidates to a more constrained system where the centre exerts much more control. Second, and relatedly, is the sub-state branch allowed to select its own leader without central interference or influence? This is an important indicator of a statewide party's attitude towards multi-level politics.

Third, a key question in relation to party organisation is finance. If sub-state parties raise most of the money they spend, then we might expect them to be in a stronger position in relation to the central party. Conversely, the central party headquarters may demand more influence in return for subsidising the sub-state branch party's activities. Finally, we have to look at how far parties are willing to tolerate policy divergence at different levels of the state. Erk and Swenden (2010: 12) suggest that sub-state differentiation in policy terms may be a sensible strategy for statewide parties. However, this runs the risk of contradictions and incoherence (Detterbeck and Hepburn, 2010: 108).

Any movement in a party's relationship with its statewide parent is thus a key focus of analysis for sub-state party change. Increasing or decreasing autonomy in particular is highly significant for the branches of statewide parties. Organisational changes may signal wider shifts in attitudes and priorities and are in part an expression of how party elites treat the territorial dimension of statewide politics. Overall, however, as with the drivers of party change, it is difficult to detect a consistent pattern of how parties respond to regional challenges. Detterbeck's (2012) detailed study of West European multi-level party politics concludes that: 'there is no uniform response of the major statewide parties towards territorial asymmetries in party competition' (Detterbeck, 2012: 240; Detterbeck and Hepburn, 2010).

Personnel

The type of candidates a party attracts and retains has a substantial impact on its behaviour (Hazan and Rahat, 2006: 109). It is strongly linked with a party's processes for formulating policy and strategy (this is particularly the case in the highly centralised Conservative Party). A party's perception in the media and public image is also determined to a great extent by its elites and how they present themselves. Thus, as Ranney (1981: 103) notes:

> It is therefore not surprising that the most vital and hotly contested factional disputes in any party are the struggles that take place over the choice of its candidates; for what is at stake in such a struggle, as the opposing sides well know, is nothing less than the control of the core of what the party stands for and does.

When selected, the power of incumbency is strong (Somit *et al.*, 1994). This can be particularly the case in parties where the 'selectorate' is composed solely of a small number of party members. This allows high-profile candidates who are already in a legislature to spend time courting individual groups and highlighting their work (Hazan and Rahat, 2006: 115–116). Hazan and Rahat (2005) find that more exclusive candidate selection procedures (involving only members or elites) are likely to be less competitive than those involving a broader section of the electorate (like party primaries).

Certain patterns of behaviour may be sustained over time therefore simply due to the difficulty of deselecting sitting members of a legislature. These elites also have a stake in defending the strategy they have pursued and the institutional arrangements that have allowed them to remain in an elected position. It is difficult for parties to change when their elites are committed to, and have a substantial stake in, the status quo. Changes in candidate selection methods are therefore a key variable in examining party change. Procedures that make the selection of candidates from certain party factions more or less likely affect internal power struggles and over time may shift a party in a new direction. In order to change a party at any level, people with new ideas must become candidates.

Policy

Bale (2008: 273) defines a measure of party change for the Conservative Party in terms of policy as 'de-emphasizing (although not ignoring completely) the issues it traditionally "owns", and ranging into enemy territory'. Programmatic change is often used as a way for parties to demonstrate internal change to voters.

For the regional branches of statewide parties, there also exists the possibility to differentiate themselves from other levels by pursuing a distinct and regionally focused policy agenda. Broadly, in comparing regional branch parties' policy platforms with their statewide parents, we can suggest three 'ideal-type' approaches:

- pursuing the same policy agenda as the statewide party;
- adapting statewide policies for regional contexts; or
- formulating distinctive regional policies that differ significantly from statewide practice.

For parties whose brands have been damaged by unpopular decisions taken when in government, it can be important to attempt to draw a line under previous controversies. Thus the deliberate disavowal of previous policy positions or the adoption of new ones which are more closely associated with a party's rivals are important means of signalling party change. For a party that was previously associated with radical free market reform, for instance, the tempering of that image by emphasising more pastoral concerns would be an important signal of a strategy of change. The Dutch Christian Democrats attempted to achieve such a change in their image (Duncan, 2007). Similarly, the UK Conservative Party under the leadership of David Cameron attempted a delicate process of distancing itself from some of the more hard-line neoliberal elements of Margaret Thatcher's legacy, whilst still acknowledging achievements that were dear to party members (Bale, 2008: 280–281; Bale, 2010; Hayton, 2012).

Examining party change

The processes of party change are complex and multi-causal. This chapter has attempted to separate out some key elements for comparative analysis and to situate the Conservatives in the wider context of political parties dealing with multi-level politics. We have also considered a number of assumptions and previous findings that we can use as a yardstick against which to measure the Scottish and Welsh Conservatives. There is a need to consider the Conservative Party explicitly as a multi-level organisation. Thus, in examining the party from the bottom up, I attempt to build on the existing literature that has considered changes at the statewide level (Bale, 2010, 2012; Hayton, 2012). In doing so, this study aims to provide a fuller account of the Conservative Party and party change.

2

The UK Conservative Party: statewide context

This chapter explores the relationship between the statewide Conservative Party and Scotland and Wales. The post-1997 Conservative Party famously took a long time to realise the extent it would have to change in order to regain office (Norris and Lovenduski, 2004; Bale, 2010; Snowdon, 2010). Before going on to examine the territorial Conservative Party in detail, we will consider the wider UK context for the changes that occurred at the sub-state level. The Scottish and Welsh Conservative parties may have been affected by wider UK-level concerns and party elites will certainly have been fully aware of developments at the top of the party. However, the same may not be said for party elites at the centre. It would be safe to assume that, beyond implementing new structures to deal with devolution, Scotland and Wales were not often at the top of the UK leader's agenda or strategy. The essential linkage functions of statewide parties make changes at the core or central level of a party of interest to studies of sub-state parties. For instance, only the UK Conservative Party can determine how much the Scottish or Welsh Conservatives can promise about further devolution of powers to the Scottish Parliament or Welsh Assembly. The decision about this most territorial of issues lies in office and opposition with the leader of the UK Conservative Party.

The Conservatives found it extremely difficult to break out of the inheritance of Thatcherism and to accept that the political strategy of the previous 18 years would not necessarily lead them back to power. For Seldon and Snowdon (2005), 1997–2005 were the Conservatives' 'barren years'. However, conclusions about party change at the UK level have to be qualified by consideration of the extent to which the party has repackaged and refocused rather than repudiated or replaced policies and attitudes from the past (Hayton, 2012).

Conservatism, unionism and statecraft

The unionist idea in the UK has evolved over time (Kidd, 2008). It has been a central feature of the political thought of the Scottish Conservative Party. The idea of Welsh unionism has been less prominent but has recently been more forcefully articulated (Melding, 2009). At the statewide level, the UK Conservative Party is also instinctively unionist in its outlook. However, in managing the territories of the UK, the central Conservative Party has subscribed to a conception of unionism that places the idea of central autonomy at its heart (Bulpitt, 1983). Thus, although the Conservative Party is generally sensitive to (and in Scotland in the period up to around 1965 may be said to have been a master of) the territorial dimension in British politics, the preservation of parliamentary sovereignty and the British Political Tradition (Richards and Smith, 2014) remains a critical component of its worldview. In its dealings with devolution, the Conservative Party since 1999 still largely subscribes to the view that the centre of British Government need not be substantially altered to accommodate Scotland and Wales. In particular, the Conservative Party has no abstract or practical conception of the federal idea of *shared rule*: the notion that sub-state units might have a formalised input into central government decisions (for instance, via more formalised intergovernmental relations or a federal second chamber).

This has been demonstrated most recently in its attitude towards Scotland's independence referendum and the subsequent proposals for further devolution (Convery, 2014a). The UK Conservative Party endorsed the Scottish Conservatives' proposals for further devolution to Scotland in the event that Scotland voted 'no'. However, these covered mainly ideas about further *self-rule* powers for Scotland over income tax and other areas (see Scottish Conservative Party, 2014). Similarly, in Wales, the St David's Day agreement envisages few changes to the central governing assumptions of Westminster beyond the creation of a new intergovernmental committee (HM Government, 2015). In negotiating the Edinburgh Agreement with the Scottish Government, David Cameron also demonstrated a pragmatic Conservative attitude towards territorial management: he would campaign for Scotland to stay in the United Kingdom, but the SNP had a right to hold a referendum and Scotland had a right to leave if it so chose. He and the Conservative Party perceived ultimately that in the event of independence 'their own polity will carry on regardless' (Keating, 2009: 369).

In short, the statewide Conservative Party has embraced devolution, and is happy to offer more of it, *to the extent that it does not interfere with the central assumptions of the Westminster model of British government*. Its strategy still chimes with Bulpitt's argument about the twentieth-century statecraft bias of the Conservative Party: 'in brief, what the Conservatives wanted to achieve in government was a relative autonomy for the centre [Cabinet and senior civil service (Whitehall)] on those matters which they defined as 'high politics' at any particular time' (Bulpitt, 1986: 27). Thus, the statewide Conservative Party is happy to grant more self-rule to Scotland and Wales, but in general does not entertain discussions of moving towards a more formally federal system or changing Westminster's unitary logic in order to accommodate a multi-level state. This attitude was encapsulated in George Osborne's budget statement in 2015 when he pointed out that the Government was delivering further powers for Scotland, as it had promised during the referendum campaign and in its manifesto. Therefore: 'Instead of complaining endlessly about process in Westminster, the SNP Scottish Government will soon have to answer the question, "You've got the powers, when are you going to use them?"' (HC Hansard, 8 July 2015, col 329). Insofar as we may infer a strategy for devolution in the statewide Conservative Party, it might be summarised as: political and economic responsibility for the devolved territories alongside an enduring commitment to traditional understandings of parliamentary sovereignty and the British Political Tradition at the centre.

Where it has strayed into changes at the centre to accommodate devolution, these have focused primarily on correcting perceived unfairness towards England through English Votes for English Laws. However, this is not located within a broader vision for the future of the UK and serves instead to further insulate the centre of British Government from potential interference from the periphery. The Conservatives cannot take this thought through to its logical conclusion in the creation of an English Parliament because it would involve the wholesale reconfiguration of the UK state. It is too early to tell if the Conservatives' plans for devolution in England via the Northern Powerhouse and other initiatives will challenge the dominance of the centre in British politics.

Where does this leave the philosophy of Conservative unionism at the centre? For Mitchell (1990: 8), Conservative unionism in relation to Scotland had three central components: 'as a social and cultural meaning, as expression of Scotland's constitutional position within the United Kingdom, and a jurisprudential meaning as the sovereignty of parliament'. In 2015, these elements are retained, but in a much thinner and less expansive way. The sovereignty of Parliament remains paramount and impedes any reimagining of the central constitution (but from a Welsh Conservative perspective, see Melding, 2009). Scotland's position in the United Kingdom was most recently defended on economic grounds in a series of interventions in the referendum campaign (see HM Treasury 2013a, 2013b, 2014). In the social and cultural sphere, any ancient attachment to Protestantism and empire has gone, but David Cameron has talked about 'our human connections – our friendships, relationships, business partnerships – they are underpinned because we are all in the same United Kingdom, and that is number one reason why we are stronger together' (Cameron, 2014).

The centre of the party is therefore not tin-eared when it comes to recognising Scottish distinctiveness and Scots' desire for further powers for the Scottish Parliament. Practically, Conservative unionism since 1997 has been shown to be pragmatic and adaptable. However, philosophically, it has withered and (beyond some economic and cultural ties) lacks a central idea of why the UK exists. Whilst reimagining the UK in the modern constitutional form of a federal state has the potential to fill this gap (Melding, 2009), this is a step that for ideological reasons the Conservative Party cannot yet take.

1997 to Hague

William Hague's leadership of the Conservative Party is widely considered to have been a tale of a talented politician who reached the top too early. Hague faced a party that had just suffered its worst electoral defeat in over a century and was still dealing with the internal splits and bitterness evident towards the end of John Major's term. For Bale (2010: 131), 'It is far-fetched to suggest that the Conservative Party that lost the election of 1997 was capable – ideologically, institutionally and individually – of moving as far to the centre as it needed to in order to stand any chance of seriously troubling Labour in 2001.'

After some perceived success at the European Parliament elections, Hague followed a strategy in 2001 that concentrated on traditional Conservative concerns and the protection of the pound (Garnett, 2003: 57). The Conservative Party made almost no progress at the 2001 general election.

For the sub-state Conservative Party, the most significant legacy of Hague's leadership was the *Fresh Future* (1998) organisational reforms. In addition to reorganising the English party's structure and the procedures for selecting the party leader, these reforms created new structures in Scotland and Wales in order to deal with devolution. In Scotland, the structure in part reflected the path-dependent processes set in train by the existence of the previously separate Unionist Party (see Chapter 5).

The new structure of the Conservative Party thus preserved and enhanced the autonomy and separate organisation of its Scottish branch. It retained formal autonomy over candidate and leadership selection, and its own separate structures through a Scottish central office. In the case of the Welsh Conservatives,

Table 2.1 Conservative Party performance at UK general elections, 1979–2010

Year	Votes	Percentage share	Number of MPs
1979	13,697,923	43.9	339
1983	13,012,316	42.4	397
1987	13,760,583	42.3	376
1992	14,093,007	41.9	336
1997	9,600,943	30.7	165
2001	8,357,615	31.7	166
2005	8,784,915	32.4	198
2010	10,726,614	36.1	307
2015	11,334,576	36.9	331

Source: Rallings and Thrasher (2009); BBC News (2010a, 2015).

a more explicitly separate party was created for the first time. However, it was considerably less organisationally distinct than in Scotland (see Chapter 4). This organisation has been described as 'confederal' (Detterbeck and Hepburn, 2010: 121).

In both cases, Hague's reforms continue the tradition of a highly centralised political party. There are high self-rule but extremely limited shared rule provisions for its sub-state branches (Fabre and Méndez-Lago, 2009: 103). Thus, while candidate and leadership selection (and to a great extent policy-making) are highly decentralised, the Scottish and Welsh parties have extremely limited input into national party decisions. There is only the provision for them to be represented on the UK party board. They have no formal right to vote or be consulted on national issues, beyond their members being able to attend the UK party conference and vote for the UK party leader.

For Detterbeck and Hepburn (2010), therefore, the Welsh and Scottish Conservative parties are 'autonomist' parties in their relationship with the UK Conservative Party. They have effective control over most sub-state matters, but do not have (and, as we will discover, mostly do not desire) substantial or formalised input into national decisions. Hague's organisational reforms entrenched this split between strong self decision-making and weak joint decision-making.

Elsewhere, following wider trends towards party democracy (see, for instance, Le Duc, 2001), the *Fresh Future* reforms also democratised the party's leadership selection procedures. This also continued a trend in the Conservative Party towards more inclusive leadership elections, having moved from a closed-door process of consultation in the 1960s towards the elections of Heath, Thatcher and Major by Conservative MPs (Kittilson and Scarrow, 2003: 65). MPs would have their say first and narrow the field down to two candidates, one of whom would then be elected by the party membership. However, beyond this democratisation of leadership selection and changes to the party's relationship with Scotland and Wales, the overall effects of *Fresh Future* were not democratising or decentralising. For Kelly (2003), the new system merely introduced a 'reformed oligarchy' that still placed enormous power in the hands of the central party leadership.

Table 2.2 Detterbeck and Hepburn's (2010: 116) typology of statewide party strategies

	Strong joint decision-making	*Weak joint decision-making*
Low autonomy for sub-state branches	Federalist	Centrist
High autonomy for sub-state branches	Modernist	Autonomist

Hague was the first Conservative leader to have to deal with having no MPs in either Scotland or Wales.[1] This presented a clear problem of party management and touched on difficult issues of legitimacy. At first Hague appointed Michael Ancram as Shadow Spokesperson for Constitutional Affairs, including responsibility for Scotland and Wales. Liam Fox later took over this post during 1998 and 1999, before he was promoted to Shadow Health Secretary.

In Wales, the party faced similar problems. At first, Jonathan Edwards was appointed as the party's chief spokesperson on Wales. After he left to seek election to the European Parliament, Nick Bourne (a future leader of the Welsh Conservative Party) took over this position. In both cases, Hague opted not to appoint shadow secretaries of state who represented English constituencies. Instead, he did the minimum to cover parliamentary duties at the UK level and ensured that there were Scottish and Welsh spokespeople underneath to handle questions on domestic matters. In any case, after 1999, Westminster ceased to be the main focus for Scottish

Table 2.3 Conservative shadow secretaries of state for Scotland, 1997–2010

Dates	Name	Constituency
June 1997–September 2001	Post vacant	
September 2001–November 2003	Jacqui Lait	Beckenham (England)
November 2003–May 2005	Peter Duncan	Galloway and Upper Nithsdale (Scotland)
May 2005*	James Gray	North Wiltshire (England)
May 2005–December 2005	Eleanor Laing	Epping Forest (England)
December 2005–May 2010	David Mundell	Dumfriesshire, Clydesdale and Tweeddale (Scotland)

* James Gray resigned after one week in the post (see p. 28).

Table 2.4 Conservative shadow secretaries of state for Wales, 1997–2010

Dates	Name	Constituency
June 1997–September 2001	Post vacant	
September 2001–July 2003	Nigel Evans	Ribble Valley (England)
July 2003–December 2005	Bill Wiggin	Leominster (England)
December 2005–May 2010	Cheryl Gillan	Chesham and Amersham (England)

Table 2.5 Leaders of the UK Conservative Party, 1997–

Dates	Name
1997–2001	William Hague
2001–2003	Iain Duncan Smith
2003–2005	Michael Howard
2005–	David Cameron

and Welsh politics. However, although it may not have made much difference at a practical level, the lack of shadow secretaries of state for Scotland and Wales was symbolically difficult for the Conservative Party. It drew attention to their weakness outside England and made their opposition to devolution even more problematic. As Major (1999: 417) concedes, the lack of Scottish MPs in any future Conservative majority government would have made devolution inevitable 'and I would have had to introduce it'.

Overall, faced with other challenges and other internal party management issues, Hague was not unduly distracted by Scotland and Wales. Having supported the campaign against devolution at the UK level, he quickly accepted the outcome and moved to restructure the party to reflect it. He was relaxed about policy divergence, particularly in Scotland, telling the Scottish party that 'you've got powers, you now deal with issues that have nothing to do with Westminster, you are absolutely in control over policy-making' (interview with MSP 9, 24 October 2012).

Duncan Smith

The 2001 Conservative Party leadership election did not feature Scotland or Wales (Alderman, 2002). Territorial issues were never at the forefront of UK party concerns during this period. Michael Portillo's pitch for his leadership campaign was a full-blooded defence of a modernisation strategy. Although David Cameron subsequently picked up many of these themes, his strategy was regarded by some commentators as too radical for the party to accept at this stage (Bale, 2010: 142; Snowdon, 2010: 85). The other candidates were Ken Clarke, David Davis, Michael Ancram and Iain Duncan Smith. After the initial ballots of MPs, Duncan Smith and Clarke emerged as the two candidates who would face a vote of party members.

Iain Duncan Smith comfortably won the leadership election, in part because Clarke's pro-European views were still considered to be unacceptable to large sections of the party. Duncan Smith began his leadership by attempting to move the party away from traditional Conservative concerns and onto new ground about public services and social justice. However, as Hayton and Heppell (2010: 432) argue,

'Duncan Smith inherited a Conservative Party that was still fundamentally divided and remained prone to internal squabbling'. Combined with his own tactical errors and lack of presentation skills, this meant that Duncan Smith was ultimately unable to deliver a full programme of change for the Conservative Party.

Under Iain Duncan Smith's leadership, therefore, the party continued mainly to concentrate on areas in which it felt comfortable, rather than challenging the Labour Party on areas where it needed to strengthen its message. However, he did begin to sketch out a broader agenda relating to social justice, partly inspired by a visit he made to Easterhouse in Scotland with David McLetchie MSP, then leader of the Scottish Conservatives.

For Scotland and Wales, this was not a period of significant change at the centre. However, for the first time since 1979, Iain Duncan Smith did appoint shadow secretaries of state for Scotland and Wales. In Scotland, one MP was returned at the 2001 general election, so Peter Duncan was an obvious choice to be Shadow Secretary of State for Scotland. In Wales, again not a single Conservative MP was returned. Duncan Smith therefore had no choice but to appoint an English MP to this post. He chose Nigel Evans, who was born and educated in Wales, but represented Ribble Valley in England. This inaugurated a trend for the UK Conservative Party of appointing shadow secretaries of state for Scotland and Wales who did not represent constituencies in those regions, but could claim to have strong links to them.

Howard

The main achievement of Michael Howard's leadership was two-fold: steadying the ship and putting in place the next generation of party leaders. Howard was installed as leader without a vote following the resignation of Iain Duncan Smith in July 2003. Although he launched his leadership with a speech that pointed in the direction of thoroughgoing modernisation (in the mould urged by figures such as Francis Maude), it became clear later that Howard would stick much more closely to traditional Conservative themes. Howard was ultimately (and understandably) unable to fully distance himself from the 1979–1997 Conservative Governments because he latterly played such a substantial part in them and overall was proud of their legacy. However, Howard managed to restore a sense of party discipline and, particularly in the House of Commons, the idea that the party had a credible candidate to be prime minister.

Howard also promoted David Cameron and George Osborne to senior posts in the shadow cabinet. This enabled them to become more well known in the party and allowed them to prove themselves as parliamentary and media performers. In particular, Cameron was in charge of drafting the 2005 general election manifesto. Howard appointed Osborne as Shadow Chancellor after the 2005 election and this is a position he has held since in opposition and government.

After he had announced his intention to resign, Howard also attempted to introduce changes to the leadership election rules. He sought to return the final say over leadership election to the party's MPs. Howard wanted to avoid another leadership election that followed the same pattern as 2011: Iain Duncan Smith was elected leader without securing the confidence of a majority of Conservative MPs. However, this reform was strongly resisted by party members (including the ConservativeHome website) and some MPs. Howard conceded that it would not be possible to change the rules and the 2005 leadership election took place under the rules introduced by William Hague (Bale, 2010: 272).

Howard's decision to downgrade the post of Shadow Secretary of State for Wales from the shadow cabinet resulted in the resignation of Nigel Evans (BBC News, 2003). Howard turned to Bill Wiggin who represented an English constituency, but had served in the Royal Welsh Fusiliers. His tenure as Shadow Secretary of State is not fondly remembered. In particular, Wiggin's stated view that the Welsh Assembly should be scrapped was at best problematic for the Welsh Conservative Party (Shipton, 2005). Peter Duncan was retained as Shadow Scottish Secretary. However, this was again outside Howard's slimmed shadow cabinet.

Peter Duncan lost his seat at the 2005 general election. In the traditional post-devolution way, therefore, Howard appointed a Scottish-born MP who represented an English constituency. However, James Gray resigned after one week in the post after reportedly suggesting that MSPs should be replaced with Scottish MPs sitting at both Holyrood and Westminster. The Scottish Conservative Party did not take kindly to this intervention (BBC News, 2005). Eleanor Laing (born in Glasgow and educated at the University of Edinburgh) took over as Shadow Secretary of State for Scotland until Cameron's election as leader.

Cameron, 'Cameronism' and territorial politics

David Cameron's leadership of the Conservative Party is widely held to have changed the party more significantly than any of the previous post-1997 leaders (Bale, 2010). He was elected on a platform of changing the look and feel of the Conservative Party (Snowdon, 2010). Both the strategy of Cameron and the circumstances came together to enable more substantial party change. David Cameron made the obvious choice for Shadow Scottish Secretary in appointing Scotland's only Conservative MP, David Mundell, to the post when he became leader. In Cheryl Gillian, however, Cameron again found an English constituency MP with Welsh connections who competently dealt with Welsh issues from 2005, and was his first Secretary of State for Wales in government.

'Cameronism' in opposition (or the style of Conservative Party change most closely associated with David Cameron) might usefully be distilled as: a broad commitment to social liberalism (particularly on areas such as gay rights and family structure); a belief that the Conservative Party's brand became toxic and that rebranding and maintaining a rebranded image is essential for the party; a commitment to what might be termed a broadly Blairite agenda in public services (no 'opting out' or up-front charges alongside choice and competition and devolution of power); and an aversion to talking about tax cuts or Britain's place in the European Union.

However, there is nothing in Cameron's approach to politics that suggests a strategic approach to the future of the UK. In particular, it seems to have a very limited constitutional scope, concentrating mainly on localism and form of human rights laws. Nevertheless, in the short term, David Cameron made clear he was willing to go to extraordinary lengths to repair the damaged Conservative brand in Scotland. He began to talk about a 'respect' agenda for Scotland and contrasted his open approach with what he portrayed as Gordon Brown's negativity about devolution (and his attitude towards Alex Salmond's SNP administration in particular). Indeed, Cameron was so willing to atone for the perceived injustices of the Conservative Governments (1979–1997) in Scotland that on one occasion he in fact went beyond the point where Scottish Conservatives felt comfortable. A Scottish party official recalls a draft of a speech Cameron was due to make in Scotland:

> I remember in January 2006, there was a speech written for the Prime Minister [Cameron] which contained a lot of stuff about Ravenscraig, poll tax, all the rest in terms of that's all wrong, and Annabel [Goldie] said you can't use that because that's not true. Scotland was in a dreadful state. Of course Ravenscraig needed to be closed. We were right. (Interview with Scottish official 4, 30 November 2012)

David Cameron signalled a clear departure from both previous Conservative and (more recent) Labour attitudes to devolution. He noted that that 'devolution is about attitudes, not just institutions'. Thus he said that: 'I would be a Prime Minister who would work constructively with any administration at Holyrood for the good of Scotland, and I would be in regular contact with the First Minister no matter what party he or she came from' (Cameron, 2009).

In addition to this accommodating tone, David Cameron has also made some significant interventions in Scottish politics. First, the Coalition Government passed the Scotland Act 2012 that largely implemented the recommendations of the Calman Commission on the future of Scottish devolution. Second, and most notably, through the Edinburgh Agreement (2012) the Prime Minister granted the Scottish Government the power to hold a referendum on independence and agreed to be bound by the outcome. He thus adopted a pragmatic approach to territorial issues (Convery, 2014a). During the referendum, Cameron joined with the other main UK party leaders to sign 'The Vow', a declaration of a timetable for further devolution to the Scottish Parliament in the event of a No vote.

Finally, Cameron's latest significant intervention has been the commencement of the Smith Commission process to find a cross-party consensus on the future of Scottish devolution. Although his announcement on the steps of Downing Street on the morning after the referendum was marred by an ill-timed foray into English

Votes for English Laws, the Smith Commission subsequently attracted the support of all of the major parties in Scotland. Cameron kept to the timetable for implementation outlined in the vow and a new Scotland Bill was announced in the first Queen's speech of his majority Government in order to implement the Smith Commission agreement.

In Wales, the agenda has also been set by commissions that the Conservatives in government have tried to pragmatically accommodate. The Coalition Agreement (2010) committed the Government to setting up a commission to consider the future of Welsh devolution. The Silk Commission published two reports (part 1 on financial powers and part 2 on the wider governmental arrangements). The first part of the report was largely implemented through the Government of Wales Act 2014. However, the tax provisions (similar in scope to the Scotland Act 2012) require another referendum in order to come into force. The political parties and the UK government agreed a way forward on the second part of the Silk report during what was known as the St David's Day process, chaired by the Secretary of State for Wales, Stephen Crabb, in November 2014. Further legislation in the 2015 Parliament will be required in order to implement this agreement, which includes transferring further powers to the Welsh Assembly and moving to a reserved powers model of devolution, like the Scottish Parliament.

Since the 1980s, Conservative prime ministers have struggled with the question of how to staff the Scottish Office. A potentially very awkward situation about the appointment of a Secretary of State for Scotland was avoided in 2010 thanks to the coalition with the Liberal Democrats (Mitchell and van der Zwet, 2010: 722; Randall and Seawright, 2012: 113). The Liberal Democrats' 11 seats in Scotland made one of their number an obvious choice for the Scotland Office during the coalition. However, in 2015 the Conservative Party came perilously close to the nightmare scenario of achieving a majority Conservative Government with no Scottish MPs. Mundell's majority was 798 in 2015. Rather than appoint an MP representing an English constituency as the junior minister in the Scotland Office, Cameron instead put his former Scottish special adviser into the House of Lords (*Holyrood Magazine*, 2015).

Conclusion

Upon hearing the news in 1990 that John Major had replaced Malcolm Rifkind as Secretary of State for Scotland, Mrs Thatcher apparently remarked: 'I was told I couldn't do that' (quoted in Torrance, 2009: 242). This mostly sums up the attitude of elites at the centre of the UK Conservative Party towards Scotland and Wales: benign incomprehension alongside a willingness to take advice. This stems from the statecraft priorities of the Conservative Party. Scotland and Wales are not essential to achieving a parliamentary majority at Westminster and can therefore be safely ignored, providing they stick to the low politics remit of the devolved institutions. As one 'Conservative aide' puts it, 'Anything in Scotland will be a bonus, but we need to be able to build a UK majority without any Scottish MPs' (quoted on ConservativeHome.com, 2011).

In the post-devolution period, Conservative statecraft in opposition had to navigate the difficult terrain of its obvious weakness in Scotland and Wales. The party's UK leaders sought mainly to avoid controversy and accommodate Scottish and Welsh concerns in a way that did not interfere with their other priorities. It would be fair to conclude, however, that Scotland and Wales (and the Scottish and Welsh Conservative parties) did not dominate their agenda. If, as in the Labour Party for instance, large numbers of Conservative MPs had represented Scottish constituencies, then this may not have been the case.

In government, the Conservative Party has supported the further devolution of powers in both the Scotland Act 2012 and the Government of Wales Act 2014. Significantly, Cameron also agreed to allow the Scottish Government to hold an independence referendum and made some generally well-judged interventions in that campaign. However, although these have been short-term successes, the Conservative Party lacks an overall strategic vision for the future of devolution in the UK. During this period, it agreed case-by-case concessions, rather than thinking about what a Conservative-designed model of devolution might look like. Thus, unless its sub-state branches fill this gap, there is a lack of strategic thinking at this level in the Conservative Party. In particular, the party appears to have no conception of the idea of *shared rule* in a multi-level state and concentrates instead on what further *self-rule* provisions might be devolved to Scotland or Wales.

In terms of party change at a UK level, the most significant shift was the transition to David Cameron's leadership. The pursuit of a clear modernisation agenda at the centre of the party with its assumptions about the damage to the Conservative Party brand will have had an impact on the party in Scotland and Wales. It will therefore be important to investigate the extent to which they accepted, rejected or pursued an alternative to the strategy outlined at the centre of the party.

Note

1 However, even in government and with MPs from Scotland and Wales, the limited pool of potential ministers for the territorial offices of state was a problem for the Conservative Party. Teddy Taylor (2008: 145) records that he felt that he was a ministerial candidate in the 1970s almost solely on the basis that he represented a Scottish constituency and was not 'an alcoholic, womaniser or illiterate'. Major (1999: 417) also worried that he would not have enough able ministers for the Scottish Office if the Conservatives won the 1997 general election.

PART II

Scotland and Wales

3

Devolution, party change and the Scottish Conservative Party

> Conservatism has played a long and historic role in Scottish politics and the Tory Party has deep roots in Scotland. However, many people do not realise this. (Margaret Thatcher, Foreword to *The Scottish Tory Party: A History* by Gerald Warner, 1988: i)

> Author: Would it be fair to say that the party has never really got over the 1997 referendum result?

> Conservative MSP: I think it is gradually getting over the referendum result. (Interview with Conservative MSP 8, 2 October 2012)

Having established the wider UK context in which it operated, this chapter now turns to examine the post-devolution Scottish Conservative Party. It finds that while the Scottish Conservatives did adapt organisationally to the external shock of devolution, they spent the following decade trying to repeat the same pre-1997 political strategy. Contrary to some assumptions in the literature about sub-state party demands for autonomy, the Scottish party in fact had more autonomy than it wanted or needed.

This chapter finds overall that the potential for party change beyond constitutions and management charts was for the Conservatives in the gift of a leadership that chose not to attempt radical change. Faced with a significant section of the party which remained hostile to devolution, the party leadership instead concentrated on more 'banal' issues of everyday parliamentary business, policy-making and campaigning (Smith, 2011), giving the impression of progress without much internal struggle. In short, the Conservative leadership in Scotland concentrated most of its energy on being a competent opposition party in a multi-party parliament. It generally ignored more fundamental questions about the party's declining support and the future of devolution. Whilst this allowed it to claim some limited policy successes during the SNP minority government (2007–2011), it was not accompanied by substantial party change in any other area.

However, the threat to the Union posed by the independence referendum was a powerful driver of change on the party's policies on devolution. This forced the party, through the second Strathclyde Commission, to come up with a Conservative vision for further powers. The party's acceptance of its radical recommendations not only placed it in a more pro-devolution camp than the Scottish Labour Party; it also encountered little of the sort of internal opposition to further powers that characterised the party's discussion of this issue since 1999.

This chapter begins by examining the history of the Scottish Conservative Party. The party still bears the mark of its original independent existence and its previous successful incarnation as the Scottish Unionist Party still informs debates in the party today. It only merged with the UK Conservative Party in 1965. This chapter then examines the potential drivers of party change for the Scottish Conservatives. Devolution prompted some organisational changes, but the most important driver of change in the post-devolution period up to 2014 was electoral defeat at the 2010 UK general election. The 2011 leadership election had the potential to install a new leader who was committed to substantial change, but in the end the party decided to elect a candidate who represented continuity. However, the external shock of the Scottish independence referendum forced the party to come up with an alternative pro-Union plan for Scotland and this, for the first time, moved the party decisively into a position where it supported further powers for the Scottish Parliament.

This chapter then examines the manifestations of party change in the post-devolution Scottish Conservatives. The party's organisation changed quite substantially after the 2010 election result following an internal report. However, no organisational changes have granted the Scottish Conservatives any further autonomy from the UK party. Similarly, policy-making has been marked by continuity and still draws substantially on the political thought of the Conservative Governments (1979–1997). There have also been no major changes in personnel that have driven party change. Change up to 2014 was confined mainly to party organisation and this was primarily driven by electoral defeat.

History of the Scottish Conservative Party

As Panebianco (1988: 50) argues, 'the characteristics of a party's origin are in fact capable of exerting a weight on its organisational structure even decades later'. The Scottish Conservative Party's previously independent history is evident in its present organisation. The Scottish Conservative Party is the oldest political party in Scotland and traces its origins to the great debates about the status of the Reformation and royal succession in the late seventeenth century. As Warner (1988: 9) explains, the word 'Tory' 'is a corruption of the Irish Gaelic *tóiridhe*, meaning "pursuer" or "brigand"; when applied by the Exclusionists to the supporters of the Catholic prince, James, it had the derogatory implication of "Irish papist bandits" or rebels'.[1]

Thus, the UK Conservative Party in Scotland exists for the most part as a result of territorial *diffusion*, rather than territorial *penetration*. Eliassen and Svaasand (1975: 16) make a distinction between those parties formed by the amalgamation of distinct units (*diffusion*) and those formed because a party at the centre has created a presence in a region from scratch (*penetration*). A party which develops through consolidation of previously separate units is likely to be more decentralised than one in which its constituent parts owe their existence and loyalty to elites at the centre (Panebianco, 1988: 51). The historical development of the Scottish Conservatives and the distinctive place of Scottish institutions within the United Kingdom have resulted in a party which throughout its existence has enjoyed a greater measure of autonomy from the centre and a separate identity. Within the Scottish party itself, divisions and associations until 1965 operated as much more independent units than their equivalents in the English Conservative Party (Urwin, 1966: 146).

The Scottish Conservative and Unionist Party is a territorial branch of the statewide UK Conservative Party (Deschouwer, 2003: 220). However, until 1965 the Scottish Conservatives were a distinct political party, the Scottish Unionist Party, which had a link to the UK Conservative Party more akin to that between the statewide CDU and Bavarian CSU in Germany. The Scottish Unionist Party itself was a coalition of different groups. In local government, for instance, many Scottish Unionists stood as Progressives in the 1950s (Seawright, 2002: 80). At the 1955 general election, in which the Unionists won 50.1 per cent of the vote in Scotland, many of its candidates stood as National Liberals.[2] It was, as Richard Finlay argues, 'the most successful organisation in Scottish politics in the period from after the Great War to the mid-1960s' (Finlay, 2012: 29).

In 1965, the Unionist Party in Scotland decided to integrate more fully with the UK Conservative Party. It dropped the distinctive Unionist Party label and became instead the Scottish Conservative and Unionist Party. Most scholars pinpoint this as

Table 3.1 Conservative electoral performance in Scotland at Westminster elections

Year	Votes	Percentage share	Number of MPs
1950*	1,222,010	44.8	31
1951*	1,349,298	48.6	35
1955*	1,273,942	50.1	36
1959*	1,260,287	47.2	31
1964*	1,069,695	40.6	24
1966	960,675	37.6	20
1970	1,020,674	38	23
1974 (February)	950,668	32.9	21
1974 (October)	681,327	24.7	16
1979	916,155	31.4	22
1983	801,487	28.4	21
1987	713,081	24	10
1992	751,950	25.6	11
1997	493,059	17.5	0
2001	360,658	15.6	1
2005	369,400	15.8	1
2010	412,855	16.7	1
2015	434,097	14.9	1

* Includes National Liberals.

Source: Rallings and Thrasher (2009); BBC News (2010a, 2015).

a key moment on the party's road to losing touch with the coalition of Scottish voters that helped it to be so electorally successful and politically relevant (Seawright, 1999; Dyer, 2001; Kidd, 2008: 22–23; Arnott and Macdonald, 2012).

The old eastern and western divisions of the party that existed before 1965 were amalgamated into a single party structure along the lines of the English party's more centralised model (Urwin, 1966; Seawright, 1999: 26–27).

Explaining Scottish Conservative decline

From the high point of the 1955 general election, the decline of the Scottish Conservative Party has been striking (Seawright, 1999). Post-devolution debates about party change in the Scottish Conservative Party are in part informed by an attempt to recapture the success of the pre-1960s. The tension between being distinctively Scottish and being loyal to the UK Conservative Party and policies will be evident throughout this chapter. In many ways, the pre-1965 Conservative Party was a quite sophisticated multi-level party before the term existed.

For Kendrick and McCrone (1989) Scottish Conservative decline can be broadly explained by two central factors: greater Scottish dependence on the public sector and the emergence of Scotland as a separate unit of economic management. The idea that Scotland faced different economic issues from the rest of the UK that required a specific policy response did not sit well with the Conservatives' increasing commitment under Thatcher to a sense of 'Britishness' in which the state was largely meant to withdraw from industrial policy. Thus Kendrick and McCrone (1989: 589) conclude that: 'The Scottish economic dimension had made Scotland an ideological category largely incompatible with Conservative English/British national rhetoric as employed by Mrs Thatcher.'

Dyer (2001) argues that the Conservatives' decline in Scotland is explained by 'a waning of the cultural conditions which produced the centre-right coalition which dominated Scottish politics, 1931–64, and its fragmentation into Conservatism, Liberalism and Scottish Nationalism' (Dyer, 2001: 30). The various factions that united under the banner of 'unionism' in Scotland created a uniquely powerful electoral constituency. However, this grouping was very much of its time. Towards the latter half of the twentieth century, 'a change in Scottish political culture ... rendered a once-powerful unionism old-fashioned and redundant' (Dyer, 2001: 32). The Conservatives' failure to reinvent themselves to adapt to the new circumstances in Scotland led to their steady drop in support.

However, Seawright (1999) rejects what he terms the 'received wisdom' about explanations for the Scottish Conservatives' decline. First, in contrast to Kendrick and McCrone (1989: 601), Seawright argues that difference in social structure between Scotland and England is not a compelling explanation for the weakening of support for the Conservatives. Although more Scottish people identify as working class than English people, Seawright (1999: 196) finds that 'social class and housing tenure trends were similar on both sides of the border, and that such trends were moving in a direction commonly thought of as beneficial to the Conservatives'.

Second, he argues that changes in religious cleavages cannot account for the Scottish Conservatives' decline. According to Seawright (1999: 196), the idea that Conservatives in Scotland benefited in the 1950s from an 'Orange' Protestant vote which has been in decline ever since is a 'shibboleth to be addressed'. His data show that there has not been a significant religious dealignment in the Scottish electorate and that 'the decline in Conservative support has occurred in those of all religions and of none' (Seawright, 1999: 109). The decline of Conservative Party support amongst Protestants can therefore be explained by the wider overall drop in support for the party. However, the data show that support for the Conservatives among Protestants remains strong. Thus, according to Seawright, 'the Conservatives are still a protestant party, simply not a very successful one' (Seawright, 1999: 197).

Third, unlike Mitchell (1990), Seawright argues that there is no link between the Conservative Party's support for devolution and its electoral success. He points out that the Conservatives might have expected to do well in Scotland in the 1970 general election after Edward Heath's 'declaration of Perth' statement on devolution. In the event, the party held its share of the vote in Scotland, but performed worse than in England. In contrast, the party did better in the elections of February 1974, following the failure of the Heath Government to implement devolution, and in 1992, when the party stood on an uncompromisingly unionist platform. Seawright (1999: 198) concludes that 'the constitutional question can neither continually swing the Scottish electorate nor permeate any one party with a Scottish consciousness or Scottish identity'.

Fourth, Seawright rejects any explanation based on the idea that Scottish people are consistently more left-wing than the English. According to his analysis of the data, 'Scots were in fact relatively more right wing in the fifties and they did not take a substantive move to the left until the 1970s. It was not the case that the party managed to match their message to the Scots' more left-learning economic and social preferences in the 1950s' (Seawright, 1999: 199). The unionist philosophy and approach that the party adopted in the 1950s was flexible with regard industrial policy and in particular to state interventions to aid declining industries. However, after Margaret Thatcher became leader of the Conservative Party, a more dogmatic 'new right' ideology began to inform the party's policies. Thus 'as the Scots took that substantive move to the left in the mid 1970s, the party simultaneously decided on a substantive move of its own towards what was hitherto regarded as extremism' (Seawright, 1999: 199).

Overall he concludes that the main explanation for Tory decline lies in drift of the Scottish Conservatives from the moderate section of the Scottish electorate from which it drew its support. Seawright's explanation is therefore more of a modification of what he described as that fourth 'received wisdom' (that the Scots are relatively more left-wing), rather than a total rejection of it: the Scots did not abandon the Scottish Tories; the Scottish Tories abandoned Scotland.

The entrenchment of an ideological shift under Thatcher combined with earlier organisational changes to create the impression that a once distinctly Scottish party had started to become 'alien' and 'English'. The internal structural changes in the party in the 1960s, including changing the name of the party from the Scottish Unionist Party to Scottish Conservative Party, helped to create the circumstances under which this negative perception could take root.

In trying to dispose of the sectarian connotations of the past once and for all, the party also ditched one of its unique selling points: its Scottish distinctiveness. According to Seawright, this further integration with the British Conservative Party, alongside an ideological shift that was perceived as abrupt and dangerous for post-industrial Scotland, created a lethal combination for the Scottish Tories. For Seawright (1999), their decline was in the end due to a mixture of ideology and image, rather than class or religion.

Regardless of its precise origins, this historical inheritance of success and decline informs present debates within the party about the future. Murdo Fraser's campaign in the 2011 leadership election drew explicitly on the pre-1965 organisation of the party to argue that a separate Scottish party merely returned the Scottish Conservatives to their natural state. All those in leadership roles within the Scottish Conservative Party have in part sought unsuccessfully to recapture the distinctive Scottish roots of the Unionist Party and use these to pursue a Scottish agenda within the UK.

Drivers of party change for the Scottish Conservatives

This section examines in turn the potential drivers of change for the post-devolution Scottish Conservative Party. After establishing the overall office-seeking bias of the UK Conservative Party and how that translated into a Scottish context, this section considers in turn: devolution and the 2014 referendum as external shocks; changes in dominant faction or leadership (including the milestone of the 2011 leadership election); and the impact of electoral defeat and decline.

This section concludes that whilst the external shock of devolution necessitated some significant organisational changes, it had a more limited impact on the party's overall Westminster bias. Similarly, although it may be argued that the issue of acceptance of the reality of the Scottish Parliament divided the Scottish Conservative Party, there did not exist strongly developed factions on either side of this debate. Although this split became more explicit and acknowledged after the 2011 leadership election, it has not become a focus for party change. Moreover, there is no evidence of significant ideological factions of the sort that might exist at the UK level (and which came to the fore in the 2005 leadership election between David Cameron and David Davis); nor is there evidence of a 'modernisers' versus 'traditionalists' split occasioned by the differing interpretations of Conservative decline and Cameron's strategy for the party.

Instead, the quiet existence of a section of the party that was opposed fundamentally to devolution – what one MSP calls the 'refuseniks' (interview with Conservative MSP 8, 2 October 2012) – acted as a brake on the leadership of the party fully engaging with the issue of devolution. This resulted in a party that concentrated on being a competent (and, to be sure, not insignificant) player in a multi-party Parliament. More fundamental issues about Scottish Conservative decline and the future of the Parliament were not discussed; instead the party engaged in what might be termed 'banal parliamentarianism' (adapted from Smith, 2011). The fact that there was little realistic prospect of ever being in office in Scotland also meant that there was no pressure on the party to try to change its policies or image so that it looked like a plausible coalition partner for the other parties.

Although Ruth Davidson won the leadership election as the continuity candidate who opposed both further devolution and a separate party, her greatest achievement as leader has been to move the party in a decisively pro-further devolution direction. The external shock of the referendum forced the Conservatives to come up with proposals for an alternative to independence. The problem of acceptance of the Scottish Parliament that dogged the Conservatives until 2011 has gradually been eroded and the radical proposals of the Strathclyde Commission (which placed the Conservatives for the first time in a generation as more ardent decentralisers than Scottish Labour) were met with hardly any opposition within the party.

Finally, this section notes for the Scottish Conservatives the importance of the *context* of electoral defeat as a driver of party organisational change. The party's results had been declining for over a decade without much effect on the party's strategy, policies or image. However, the disappointing results in Scotland of the 2010 general election had a much greater impact because they occurred at a time when the English and Welsh parties were recovering and because the Scottish party contributed to the Conservatives' failure to be able to govern alone at Westminster.

External shocks: devolution and the 2014 referendum

In the post-war era, the Scottish Conservative Party shared with the UK Conservative Party an overriding desire to be in power. This was the product not only of a highly majoritarian two-party system, but also of a deeply engrained culture in the Conservative Party itself. John Ramsden (1998: 495) describes 'the party's quite remarkable facility for adaptation and, closely allied to this, its appetite for power, often indeed its readiness to subordinate all other considerations to that one objective'. Robin Harris (2011: 4) observes that, 'The Conservative Party exists, has always existed and can only exist to acquire and exercise power, albeit on a particular set of terms.' In short, the UK Conservative Party is an office-seeking party *par excellence*: 'its public identity and its own self-image are bound up with being a party of government' (Ball, 2005: 1). Opposition is considered as 'an aberrant state of affairs rather than part of the normal cycle' (Ball, 2005: 1).

Before 1999, the only way for the Conservative Party to be in power in Scotland was to ensure that it had a majority at the UK level. The sights of Conservative elites and activists were therefore focused firmly on Westminster. The priority was to ensure that a Conservative Secretary of State for Scotland was appointed. In comparative terms, this is quite unusual and is a feature of the way in which administrative devolution in the UK developed (Mitchell, 2003). Although gradually more Scottish domestic policy came to be decided by ministers and civil servants in Edinburgh, the only way to access these levers of power was through Westminster. The Westminster bias of the Scottish Conservatives is therefore entirely reasonable and understandable. The more the Conservatives struggled in local government in Scotland, the more important it became.

This attitude is also partly due to the nature of unionist political thought in the Conservative Party and in Scotland. The priority of Westminster office was a goal that required little articulation or justification. The institutions of the Union were for Conservatives in Scotland the natural place in which to invest their time and energy. Unlike for the other main Scottish parties, they were never perceived as illegitimate or the source of a threat to Scottish distinctiveness. For the Conservatives, they were not English institutions; instead, they formed part of the institutional architecture of a UK 'fifth nation' (Rose, 1982: 3; Aughey, 2011) to which Scotland had privileged access (articulated in: HM Government, 1993; Lang, 2002: 202–206; Kidd, 2008: 35). Moreover, as Kidd (2008: 25) points out, 'The Union occupied a position of such unchallenged dominance in Scottish life between about 1750 and 1970 that there was no need to make a vigorous case on its behalf.'

However, since the political element of the Scottish Question sharpened in the 1970s, the Conservatives found it extremely difficult to incorporate their understanding of unionism with a sense that Scottish (political and policy) identity could only be fully preserved and enhanced through new Scottish political institutions. Thus, as Mitchell (1990: 12) argues, 'The problem for unionism has been that, in maintaining a distinctive Scottish aspect, the danger always existed that a demand to incorporate a democratic component would be made or even that the Union should be abandoned. [For Conservatives] the defence of the Union comes first, before the retention of the Scottish aspect whenever the question is put.' In the post-devolution period, it is difficult to argue that this is not still the case for the Conservatives. The external shock of devolution did provoke the kind of soul-searching necessary to fundamentally change the party's conception of unionism (Mitchell and Convery, 2012). It did not prompt any significant figure in the party to ask stark questions along the lines of: have we been anti-Welsh? (Melding, 2009: 136). Instead, the Conservatives in Scotland allowed their unionist ideology to wither, becoming gradually shriller and less tolerant (Kidd, 2008: 303).

Thus, the sense of the priority of Westminster office proved to be so deeply entrenched across the whole party that after 1999 it was extremely difficult to reorient its priorities towards being in power in the Scottish Parliament. Indeed, anecdotally, according to one party official in 2012, 'if I went round hard-core Conservatives, knock on the door, they'll say, "that joke of a Parliament". They'll still say it', with some members adding for good measure, 'and I was better off under the poll tax' (interview with Scottish official 4, 30 November 2012). Thus, although devolution was undeniably an external shock for the Scottish Conservatives, it had a more limited impact on the party's internal culture of priorities.

There is a long tradition of Scottish Conservative MSPs standing for Westminster seats. South of Scotland MSP David Mundell became the MP for Dumfriesshire, Clydesdale and Tweeddale in 2005. Ben Wallace, a North East regional MSP elected in 1999, became the MP for the English constituency of Lancaster and Wyre in 2005. In addition, Phil Gallic MSP stood in Ayr in 2001 and Alex Johnstone MSP and John Lamont MSP stood for Westminster seats in both 2005 and 2010 (Torrance, 2012: 102). John Lamont stood for the same House of Commons seat in 2015.

When the author put it to a Scottish Conservative MSP in 2012 that the Scottish Conservative Party had never got over the 1997 referendum result, he paused before replying that, 'I think it is gradually getting over the referendum result.' He continued:

> There are a lot of people in the party who would just not accept that it is over and that the way that we had done things was not going to be the way that it would have to be in the future. In fairness, there were some who did say that and came up with quite radical ideas, shall we say, but there were others, principally people who were actually not in the Parliament, but who could never get their heads round where we were in this regard. (Interview with Conservative MSP 8, 2 October 2012)

Despite repeated commitments to the reality of devolution made in forewords to manifestos and leaders' speeches, the Conservative Party in Scotland found it extremely difficult both philosophically and practically to accept that the Scottish Parliament was now the major forum in Scottish politics to which most of their attention should be devoted. Ironically, for the same MSP, devolution may in fact have acted as an impediment to substantial party change in other areas. He poses an interesting counter-factual to capture the mood of some in the party:

> I would say that it's a faction of the membership. It all goes back to this fundamental issue of the Scottish Parliament, what was it for, etc., etc. I mean, I don't think there would have been anything like the same problem had there not been a Scottish Parliament, if Labour had just won the election and that was it, you know, and we would have got used to focusing without a Scottish Parliament, etc., etc. Now, we might not have won any elections any earlier, but we would have gone with that. The fact of the matter is that the Scottish Parliament has changed the characteristics in this respect and we have been slower than many others to actually catch up with that. (Interview with Conservative MSP 8, 2 October 2012)

Devolution never therefore succeeded in providing the kind of shock necessary to move the party forward into recognising the Scottish Parliament as the important institutional expression of Scottish identity to which the Conservatives had to seem wholeheartedly committed. This acted as a major brake in other areas:

> some of the difficulty was because we are … we are in a situation where we have our clump of supporters who are no great fans of the Scottish Parliament at all. They basically don't really want you to do anything other than kind of ignore it if you can. And then you have got other people who are actually more alive to the possibilities of what we could do, and if you are the leader in that situation, you have got to try and then balance up the respective interests. I would say that in 2003 we did that by focusing on some of the peripheral issues, what in the grand scheme of things have turned out to be peripheral issues, but things like, you know, the cost of the parliament building, isn't this a scandal, etc? And there was a huge amount of time and energy went into focusing on the costs of the parliament, but of course that was never going to be anything other than a peripheral issue. I mean, by 2005 it was all basically done and dusted and, you know, we were where we were. So I think probably in some respects if I had a failing it would be that I probably did not move the party on far enough, fast enough in that particular time, but, you know, that's the way you see it. (Interview with Conservative MSP 8, 2 October 2012)

Conservatives had also to deal with the fact that the pursuit of office was not a realistic priority for them in the Scottish Parliament. They simply saw no prospect of being in coalition with the other parties. This potential driver of change was therefore absent. Moreover, according to one MSP:

> We knew a lot of the Conservative voters in the early years of this parliament had never voted for the Scottish Parliament in the first place and therefore it was a hard enough sell for us to get them to come out and vote at all in a Scottish Parliament election. If we had said, you know, given it was a PR system, come out and vote for us so we can go into coalition with the Labour Party or the SNP, that would have been even worse and put more of them off, so sticking to very core Conservative messages, we thought, was the best way to try and motivate our voters, who we knew would come out in a Westminster election, to come out also in the Scottish Parliament elections. (Interview with Conservative MSP 1, 6 March 2012)

This uneasy standoff at a national level was also reflected at a local level in Smith's (2011) ethnographic study of how the local Dumfries and Galloway Conservative Party attempted to cope with the impact of devolution and the widespread antipathy towards the party. Smith spent a year embedded in the local party, leading up to the Scottish Parliament elections of 2003. He concludes that the party busied itself with what he terms 'banal activism' in order to try to maintain a sense of purpose and unity in a difficult organisational and political climate (Smith, 2011: 131). Thus the focus of activists' lives became the production of the *In Touch* electoral leaflet and the processes surrounding it. In short, 'the busy work of the banal activist had propelled and sustained them during the campaign' (Smith, 2011: 132). In the absence of a compelling national agenda to follow, the local party had to find its own way of keeping together and running a campaign. In the end, a reasonable result was achieved, but this represented more the management of difficult circumstances, rather than a Conservative renaissance. Smith concludes that the Conservatives in Scotland have reached the end of the line with this sort of muddling through:

> Buffeting against the limits of what they can achieve through their focus on local level activism and issues, they have successfully postponed the kind of vexing philosophical and policy debates that would have no doubt exacerbated internal divisions but remain essential to any attempts by the Party to argue that it has undergone change and renewal. (Smith, 2011: 135–136)

Thus, the external shock of devolution did not result in the Scottish Conservatives refocusing their office-seeking instincts from Westminster to Edinburgh or recalibrating their philosophy of unionism to incorporate a Conservative vision for the Scottish Parliament (despite working hard for several important causes within it – see, for instance, Douglas-Hamilton, 2009). Instead, the comfort the party found in 'banal activism' (or what might be termed 'banal parliamentarianism' at the national level) and the steady results it has produced against a background of low expectations enabled the Scottish Conservatives until at least 2010 to avoid facing up to more fundamental questions. This resembles a path-dependent process of positive feedback: banal activism allows the party to hold together and claim just enough electoral success to justify ignoring more controversial issues on which significant disagreement bubbles just below the surface.

Overall, the force of devolution as a driver of party change was blunted by a deeply engrained conception of unionism and the idea that governing at Westminster remained the Scottish Conservatives' priority. While devolution could certainly act as a driver for *organisational* changes, it had a much smaller impact on the Scottish Conservatives' certain idea of a central purpose. Fundamentally, it could not reorient the Scottish Conservatives' priority from contributing seats to a Westminster Conservative majority to being in government in the Scottish Parliament. Such a change in priority would have had the potential to drive other substantial changes in policy and leadership before 2011.

However, the 2014 referendum on Scottish independence had a much more decisive impact on the Scottish Conservatives. The Scotland Bill that emerged from the Calman Commission was quickly overtaken by events. Ironically, the defining achievement thus far of Ruth Davidson's leadership (considering the devolution-sceptic platform on which she campaigned for that post) has been to move the Scottish Conservatives towards accepting a pro-devolution stance. Along with the other political parties in Scotland, she set up a commission to consider what further powers could be devolved to Scotland in the event of a continuation of the Union after the referendum. Lord Strathclyde's Commission proposed that the Scottish Parliament be given control over all income tax receipts in Scotland (Scottish Conservative Party, 2014). Apart from the Liberal Democrats, the Scottish Conservatives had the most radical proposals of any statewide party for further devolution to Scotland.

It was hugely significant that there was hardly any dissent in the party about these plans. The referendum forced the Scottish Conservatives to face up to the challenge of marrying their economic liberalism with their attitude towards the constitution (Mitchell and Convery, 2012). The choreography of the referendum and its aftermath helped to force the Scottish Conservatives into clarifying and rallying round an alternative vision for Scotland that did not involve independence. The idea of the Union being in danger acted as a potent driver to consider alternatives and demonstrate to Scots tempted to vote Yes that remaining in the UK did not mean no change.

The Conservatives being in government in Westminster also contributed to this pressure. The UK Government was forced to have a position on what would happen after the referendum. The Conservative Party therefore needed a clear message at both levels about what it would do if it were still in power in 2015. Moreover, after the referendum result, the Scottish Conservatives were immediately forced into the Smith Commission process to hammer out a cross-party deal on further devolution. The party could not logically disown an agreement that it had been instrumental in formulating. In the end, the processes around the referendum (and particularly the Conservatives' place in the UK Government) forced the Scottish Conservatives' hand. It was much more difficult to be ambivalent about the Scottish Parliament or more powers for it when it seemed that such a position (far from preserving the Union) now risked the future of the United Kingdom. The existential threat of independence was a much more potent driver of party change in the Scottish Conservatives than the introduction of devolution.

Change in dominant faction or leadership

For one official, the Scottish Conservative Party had after 1997 'become not a very political organisation in a sense' (interview with Scottish official 2, 2 November 2011). There were no major ideological or policy splits of any note in the post-devolution party (although there was one principled resignation over fisheries policy). The only change of leadership before Ruth Davidson's election in 2011 did not bring to power a new faction or leader within the party with a radically different agenda. There were no major ideological factions in the Scottish Conservatives, except the gaping philosophical fault-line that ran through the party about devolution itself. This may in part be explained by the fact that the main economic and fiscal levers remained at Westminster. Overall, changes in leadership or faction were not a central driver of party change.

From the 1980s to 2011: dormant factions?

As Finlay (2004: 370) has argued, 'one of the features of the Scottish Conservative Party was that it had missed out on the Thatcher ideological revolution that had swept through its southern counterpart'. With the exception of Michael Forsyth, the Conservative secretaries of state for Scotland in the 1980s and 1990s were either old-style patrician Tories who had little time for ideology (George Younger); associated explicitly with the left-leaning Scottish Tory Reform Group (Malcolm Rifkind); or generally regarded as Conservative moderates (Ian Lang). Ideological debates between different factions of the party tended to play out on a UK level. The Scottish party's political leadership was more concerned with protecting Scottish public spending and securing Scotland's privileged access to the UK centre (Lang, 2002). This lack of an overall strategic plan contributed to the party's gradual decay during the 1980s (Stewart, 2009: 49). Even Michael Forsyth's tenure as Secretary of State did not produce a belated Thatcherite revolution in the Scottish Office (Torrance, 2006: 326–335).

In the post-devolution period, there were no significant changes in the ideological factions that led the Scottish Conservative Party. First, decisions about the main ideological direction of the party were taken at a UK level. The Scottish Conservative Party was not on the whole dissatisfied with this situation. Indeed, it could be argued that from at least the early 1990s the party pursued an explicitly 'assimilationist' strategy which meant that it increasingly saw itself 'as linked by an umbilical cord to the UK Conservative Party. And it didn't see itself separately' (interview with Scottish official 2, 2 November 2011).

Second, the limited economic and fiscal levers in the hands of the Scottish Parliament meant that significant ideological debates about, for instance, the proper balance between the state and the market were not essential for the Scottish Conservative Party. Debates (such as there were any during this period) and ideological positions were concerned with valance issues about the running of public services devolved to Scotland. Major splits about domestic policy direction are not a feature of the post-devolution Scottish Conservatives.

Third, it is difficult to discern any major ideological difference among either the three post-devolution leaders of the Scottish Conservative Party or its MSPs. It would be unfair to characterise any of them as true-believing Thatcherites in the mould of Michael Forsyth, for instance. David McLetchie (1999–2005) pursued a continuation of much of the pre-1997 Conservative agenda within the limits of the Scottish

Table 3.2 Leaders of the Scottish Conservative Party, 1999–2013

Dates	Name
1999–2005	David McLetchie
2005–2011	Annabel Goldie
2011–	Ruth Davidson

Parliament's authority. Thus, there would be a continuation of the NHS internal market, but the party set its face against tuition fees for university students (Scottish Conservative Party, 1999). Annabel Goldie (2005–2011) mostly continued in the same vein, with nods towards greater public service choice and mutualisation of Scottish Water, alongside clear spending commitments for pensioners and health visitors (Scottish Conservative Party, 2011). During the Scottish Conservatives' first-ever contested leadership election, Ruth Davidson's campaign website contained standard centre-right fare on school standards and choice in pubic services with which few Conservatives could disagree (Convery, 2014b). Scottish Conservative domestic policy in the post-devolution period is not the subject of the kind of debates that might allow the identification of those clearly on the 'left' or 'right' of the party.

The 2011 Scottish Conservative leadership election

Instead, the major split in the Scottish Conservative Party does not concern economic policy, public services or even Europe: it is about devolution itself. However, this split did not come to a head until the 2011 leadership election. Only at this point do we see the emergence of two distinct factions of any significance in the Scottish Conservative Party (although they result from tensions which can be detected from the beginning of devolution). The 2011 leadership election was the first contested leadership election for the post-devolution Scottish Conservatives. It thus provided the opportunity to discuss the future of the party in public.

The two factions that emerged concerned both the constitution of the UK and the Conservative Party. Broadly, on the one hand were those who felt that devolution had gone far enough and that the Scottish Conservatives should remain integrated with the UK Conservative Party; on the other were those who believed that the Scottish party had to become much more visibly autonomous and that it should be open to leading the debate on further devolution to Scotland.

The contest was dominated by arguments about Murdo Fraser's leadership pitch. He argued that 'there is no future for the Scottish Conservative and Unionist Party in its current form' (Fraser, 2011) and that the party should disband and reform itself as a new centre-right Scottish party. Like the Unionist Party, this would be a separate entity, but would probably nevertheless have MPs who took the Conservative whip at Westminster. The other three candidates (Ruth Davidson, Jackson Carlaw and Margaret Mitchell) declared their opposition to this plan and proposed reforming the Scottish Conservatives within their present structure.

The candidates were also split on the question of the future of the UK. While Murdo Fraser was open minded about further devolution, both Davidson and Carlaw declared that they viewed the Scotland Bill (based on the report of the Calman Commission) as the last word on further powers for the foreseeable future. Famously, Davidson declared that it was a 'line in the sand'. Margaret Mitchell went further and declared her opposition to some aspects of the then Scotland Bill.

Ruth Davidson won the contest, which revealed two broad factions within the Scottish Conservatives. There were those who supported Murdo Fraser's plan for a separate party (the majority of the MSP group and a significant number of party members) and those who still took a dim view of further devolution and wished to maintain the integrated UK Conservative Party (many ordinary members and Margaret Mitchell MSP).

Ruth Davidson was described by the media as a lesbian who enjoys kick-boxing (see, for instance, *Holyrood Magazine*, 2011). However, despite her being on paper a symbolic change for the party, by standing so explicitly against Murdo Fraser's plan she became in fact the continuity or no-change candidate. Had Murdo Fraser been elected and separated the Scottish Conservative Party from the UK party, there would have been a strong case for saying that a change in leadership and dominant faction had been a central driver for party change. However, by electing Ruth Davidson, the Scottish Conservatives opted to continue along broadly the same post-devolution path, but with a leader who represented a change of generation and perhaps a change in attitudes to some social issues. It was not at all clear at this time that Ruth Davidson (perhaps forced by events) would subsequently in office achieve Murdo Fraser's goals: to move the party decisively in a pro-devolution direction.

Impact of UK factionalism on the Scottish Conservatives

As Verge and Gómez (2011: 3) point out: 'factional conflict is potentially aggravated by territorial conflict between party levels'. The UK's electoral system and the party's history have resulted in a Conservative Party that is a broad coalition of different interests. In the post-war Conservative Party, we may detect a distinction between those broadly on the left and the right of the party. The most significant factional split that began to emerge in the UK Conservative Party in the post-devolution period was between the traditionalists and the Cameroons (Bale, 2010; Snowdon, 2010).

However, it is notable that the Scottish Conservative Party managed largely to insulate itself from wider debates in the Conservative Party about where it was all going so wrong, particularly after the election of David Cameron. The absence of any contested leadership elections until 2011 certainly contributed to this lack of introspection. However, at a much deeper level the lack of factionalism and discussion at the Scottish level also demonstrated the extent to which members of the Scottish Conservative Party saw the UK party as the appropriate forum for such discussions. It also demonstrated the extent to which the Scottish Conservatives had found a comfortable stasis in which deeper questions were parked in order to concentrate on the more manageable (and achievable) goals of the discharging of the functions of a competent political party (see Smith, 2011). Around 15–20 MSPs gives a political party in Scotland access to attractive parliamentary resources both for the party machine and its elected representatives.

Yet the 'Cameroon' diagnosis of the problems for the Conservative Party arguably applied more to Scotland than to any other part of the UK. If Lord Ashcroft (2005: 4) felt compelled to state bluntly that the UK 'Conservative Party's problem is its brand', then it would be difficult to overstate the extent of the cultural phenomenon that hatred of the Conservative Party brand had become in Scotland by 1997. Indeed, Hassan (2012: 77) argues that: 'in Scotland anti-Toryism and anti-Thatcherism are still the current defining political narratives, with a backstory about the 1980s, what Scotland is, why we are different and what our politics and values are today'. The Scottish Conservatives chose largely to ignore this fact. When confronted with questions about whether the Scottish Conservatives needed to detoxify their brand, party elites in the main questioned the very premise of such an analysis. For instance, one MSP in Scotland stated:

> by and large people don't talk about a detoxified Labour brand, I mean they have just lost an election. But we seem to spend our whole time talking about a detoxified Conservative brand, so I am not convinced that the problem exists in the way that it has been presented and there is no obvious evidence to my mind that it exists, other than it feeding on itself. (Interview with Conservative MSP 8, 2 October 2012)

Another MSP was also unimpressed with appeals to the concept of brand detoxification:

> It's not a word I ever used. One colleague in particular used it and commentators picked it up, and it wasn't an adjective that found favour with me because I felt that the only way to represent the Conservatives and try and emerge from this somewhat unwelcome umbrella of what I describe as a kind of generic hostility, which varied. (Interview with Conservative MSP 9, 25 October 2012)

Instead:

> about representation or rebranding or re-imaging, I felt one of the best ways of addressing that was to actually literally give people the proof of the pudding in the eating. In other words, don't judge us on your perceptions based over 30 years; judge us on our achievements based over the last four years. Now I think we made some headway with that. (Interview with Conservative MSP 9, 25 October 2012)

For another MSP, the idea of 'brand detoxification' was a rather tawdry activity for marketing consultants, and not the real work of a serious political party (interview with Conservative MSP 4, 10 April 2012). There was also a feeling post-2005 that any branding issues could be sorted out at a UK level and that the results would automatically follow in Scotland (interview with Conservative MSP 5, 17 April 2012). Thus, there has been little opportunity for a faction against Cameronism to form in Scotland because nobody has yet tried to provide or support it.

During this period, thinkers in the UK Conservative Party began to articulate the kind of diagnosis and analysis which would form the basis of Cameron's modernisation plan (see, for instance, Vaizey et al., 2001). Lord Ashcroft's analysis (2005) became particularly influential. The Conservative Party in Scotland largely ignored this debate. In 2006, one senior UK Conservative commented: 'I'm not really sure we know what to make of them, really. They're certainly not very close to what we're trying to do here' (quoted in Torrance, 2012: 103). Similarly, recalling the 2010 general election campaign, George Bridges remarked that 'the organisation up there was completely ramshackle. They didn't understand what we were trying to do at all and I had almost no control up there as Director of Campaigns. It was a complete struggle, so they employed an extra person for us to liaise with but it didn't make much of a difference' (quoted in Snowdon, 2010: 247).

One of the central reasons for this lack of engagement with the idea of a problem with the Conservative brand was the manner in which senior Scottish Conservatives read polling data. There was a perception in Scottish Conservative Central Office and elsewhere in the party that it was hardly worth reaching out to new voters when the party could not even attract all of the Conservative Party identifiers in Scotland. When the author asked a party official about Lord Ashcroft's analysis of the problems of the Conservative Party, he revealed something significant about strategic electoral thinking in the party up to 2010 and the reasons why 'brand detoxification' never really found a home in Scotland:

> The brand issue? Well, I think it's worse in Scotland because the brand actually does better. So if you, if you imagine a poll, if we were to do a poll now and say, which party do you identify with across the UK, about 26–27 per cent of the people in Scotland would say they identify with the Conservative Party and regard that as the party which is closest to their values. Ask them how they are going to vote, and that falls to sort of, whatever, 14, 15 usually. So actually, so you've got that gap, and then in England and Wales, it's then getting from the 33 per cent, 34 per cent of people in England and Wales who say they identify with the UK Conservative Party up to the 40 per cent to get us a majority, so the big issue there is toxicity, the NHS, and things that swing these people. We've got an issue where we are not even getting the people who, even toxic as we are, who still recognise that party as being their party ... between 2005 and 2010, we got into a position where we were never really thinking about the next level of voters to go through, because we have always got this situation that there is this bunch of voters who won't vote for us, most of whom probably vote SNP, who should be voting for us and identify with us. (Interview with Scottish official 4, 30 November 2012)

The perceived existence of these 'missing Conservatives'[3] had a significant impact on strategic thinking within the Scottish Conservative Party:

> I'd like to think it was as strategic as that, but it wasn't. I think in the first decade, I mean between 1999 and 2005 it was continuing to exist. I think between 2005 and now, you know, at every strategy meeting or anything I am ever at, the key group we work on is those who should be voting Tory but aren't. (Interview with Scottish official 4, 30 November 2012)

The party primarily sought out lost sheep, rather than new voters. Combined with the idea that any improvements to the Conservative brand could be achieved at a UK level, this meant that (particularly post-2005) there was no faction in the Scottish Conservative Party that promoted a radical reappraisal of the Conservative brand until the 2011 leadership election.

Electoral defeat

Devolution required the Conservative Party to change. However, this study argues that devolution was not the main driver of party change for the Scottish Conservatives. Instead, before the 2014 referendum, the greatest driver of change was electoral defeat at Westminster elections. This is because electoral defeat at the UK level in 1997 and 2010 struck at the heart of what many Scottish Conservatives saw as their primary purpose. Boin (2004: 168) argues that 'a crisis occurs when the institutional structure of a social system experiences a relatively strong decline in legitimacy as its central service functions are impaired or suffer from overload'. Whilst the results of the 2001 and 2005 general elections could be explained away by wider UK Conservative weakness, the 2010 general election result tested to destruction assumptions about the importance of returning to power at Westminster. As the Sanderson Commission (2010: 8) notes: 'There is no doubt that the Scottish Conservatives' lack of progress since the Conservative defeat in the 1997 general election contributed to the lack of an outright Conservative victory in the general election this May.' This stark

Table 3.3 Scottish Conservative performance at Scottish Parliament elections

Constituency

Year	Votes	Percentage share	Number of MSPs
1999	364,425	15.6	0
2003	318,279	16.6	3
2007	334,743	16.6	4
2011	276,652	13.9	3

Regional list

Year	Votes	Percentage share	Number of MSPs
1999	359,109	15.4	18
2003	296,929	15.5	15
2007	284,005	13.9	13
2011	245,967	12.4	12

Source: Rallings and Thrasher (2009); Scottish Parliament (2011).

realisation resulted in the wider crisis of legitimacy in structures and strategy that prompted the party in 2010 to appoint a commission to examine further organisational change. The all-too-familiar lack of progress in the 2007 Scottish Parliament elections (nearly a decade after the introduction of the Strathclyde reforms) did not result in such a fundamental reappraisal of what the party was doing.

Reflecting on the 2005 and 2010 general elections, one party official recalls that:

> We didn't come out of the 2005 general election feeling dreadfully upset. I think we come out of it thinking that it's a shame that Peter Duncan lost obviously, but one for one. And we almost won Angus, we almost won Perth and North Perthshire, we did better in Eastwood than we expected, so therefore there is a path one can see us going down and once we win at Westminster again we will win all these areas. (Interview with Scottish official 4, 30 November 2012)

Similarly, results of the first Scottish Parliament elections proved for most in the party to be a pleasant surprise following their disastrous Westminster results (interview with MSP 8, 2 October 2012; interview with MSP 9, 24 October 2012). However, the 2010 general election generated a different response: 'the fact we came out with exactly what we had, I think, was just a real shock for the party and that's where the Sanderson thing came from' (interview with Scottish official 4, 30 November 2012). Another former official puts it like this:

> Sadly, I think there was a bit of an excuse that, as long as the party was doing badly down south, it didn't expose the party up here to the same extent. It can be put down to a general malaise in Conservatism and it was worse here because we were starting from a lower base. So I think it was only when the party started to pick up there and we didn't, that then I think the issues of 'hang on a minute, is there not something more fundamental that is holding us back?' (Interview with Scottish official 2, 2 November 2011)

The idea that the failure of the Scottish Conservatives had directly harmed the chances of forming a Conservative Government at Westminster is a powerful one in a party that still set great store by regaining office at the UK level. Thus, defeat in this context drove change because it tested a particular strategy and set of assumptions to destruction (Bale, 2012: 216). The 2010 election result led to the establishment of the Sanderson Commission, which recommended party organisational reform. In Janda *et al.*'s (1995: 182–183) typology of electoral defeats, the 2010 general election for the Conservatives may be considered *calamitous*: a decisive rejection of the party or its policy stance or the clear endorsement of an electoral rival (primarily the Labour Party).

However, the 2015 general election was interpreted using a different lens. Once again the party failed to make any progress in terms of seats, returning only David Mundell in Dumfriesshire, Clydesdale and Tweeddale. The overall context of the SNP landslide and the UK Conservative majority masked this disappointment and it did not spark major discussions in the party of the sort that occurred after 2010.

The 2015 election may be characterised for the Scottish Conservatives as *disappointing* rather than calamitous. It has not sparked major debates about further party change.

Political opportunity structure

If a set of changes comes to be considered as essential for a party to regain office, then this can act as a powerful driver for change. This driver of change was absent for the Scottish Conservatives because of the structure of political opportunities created by the Scottish Parliament electoral system and the Scottish party system. The Mixed Member Proportional (MMP) electoral system means that a coalition government in Scotland is a likely outcome. Thus, in order to be in power the Conservatives would have to be a viable coalition partner for one of the other parties. In the post-devolution period, this was unlikely for several reasons. First, the other parties were in 1997 united in their opposition to the Conservative Government. In the case of Labour and the Liberal Democrats, they had been brought together in the Scottish Constitutional Convention to formulate a plan for devolution that the Conservatives stridently opposed. The Scottish National Party, which was also archly anti-Conservative, had internal rules stipulating they could not work with the Conservative Party. Second, even leaving to one side the other parties' aversion to working with a party they considered a common enemy, their combined strength meant that they did not even need to consider doing so. The other parties could ignore the Conservatives and still combine the numbers necessary to form a coalition administration in the Scottish Parliament.

The possibility of government, therefore, seemed a very remote one. If there had been a realistic chance of being in a coalition government, then this could have acted as a driver, for example, to change the party's image or ensure its manifesto contained an implementable agenda. However, even had there been such an opportunity, it is not clear that the Scottish Conservatives considered government in Scotland a high enough priority to make the changes necessary to seem like a viable coalition partner for other parties that considered themselves anti-Tory.

Manifestations of party change

In the post-devolution Scottish Conservative Party, the main manifestation of party change until 2014 affected party organisation. This was prompted by the results of the 2010 general election in Scotland. On all of the other indicators identified for examination in the analytical framework (territorial organisation autonomy, policy-making and personnel) there were no significant changes until the party's emphatic embrace of further devolution in 2014. Instead, the party has preferred to concentrate on being a competent opposition player in a multi-party parliament. In particular, despite some of the literature pointing towards sub-state parties' demands for further autonomy (see, for instance, Hopkin, 2003: 230; Van Houten, 2009: 140–141; Detterbeck, 2012: 42), the Scottish Conservatives' position in the post-devolution period could never be characterised as straining at the leash. The assimilationist strategy it adopted was not as a result of any pressure or lack of autonomy from the UK Conservative Party.

Party organisation

One of the most obvious and easy ways for a party both to adapt and be seen to be adapting to new circumstances is to reform its internal structures. However, organisational changes do not necessarily accompany changes in a party's attitudes, policies or power structures. It is easier to come to terms with devolution in an organisational chart than in reality. Organisational reform in the Conservative Party is often displacement activity that distracts attention from more pressing but difficult issues (Ball, 2005: 13; see also Kelly, 2003). This has been the experience of the Scottish Conservatives through their two major post-devolution internal restructuring exercises: the Strathclyde Commission (1998) and the Sanderson Commission (2010).

The Reforms of the Strathclyde Commission (1998)

It is commonly understood that the Conservatives were 'wiped out' in Scotland at the 1997 general election. In terms of parliamentary representation this is certainly true. The Conservatives lost all 11 Scottish MPs and suffered a steep decline in vote share. However, organisationally, the party of the government of Scotland for the previous 18 years remained largely intact. That is to say that it retained the kind of constituency and national structures required to service up to around 20 MPs at the same time as governing. The Conservative Party in 1997 did not approach the issue of party organisation with anything like a clean slate. One party official recalls:

> Inevitably if you are at, you know, as we were, especially before 1999, at 6, 7 per cent in the opinion polls, and you still have the apparatus of a significant political party, so, you know, losing all the MPs in 1997, you still had whatever, I don't know what the membership would have been in 1997, probably about 40,000 people, and the money and everything else, and these people are horrified by what's happening, but things just continue as normal, the associations continue as normal, they select candidates, so everything just keeps going on. And so, you know, if there had been a real wipe-out in 1997, you would have had a position where you could do what you wanted because there was nothing to stop you, but actually, we went to a conference immediately afterwards, 1,200 people at the conference, very well-attended conference, absolutely determined to oppose devolution. So everything just continues as it is. And I do think that that in terms of strategy it made it very difficult. (Interview with Scottish official 4, 30 November 2012)

It was in this context that Scottish Conservatives asked Lord Strathclyde to chair a commission to recommend organisational changes to adapt the party to the challenge of the Scottish Parliament. The pre-1997 structure of the Scottish Conservatives maintained a split between the voluntary, professional and parliamentary wings of the party. Party members were technically not members of the Conservative Party, but of the Scottish Conservative and Unionist Association (SCUA).

The structure of Strathclyde's recommendations therefore still bears the mark of not only the pre-1997 organisation, but also the bias towards securing power at the Westminster level. Although the Strathclyde Commission prompted some significant organisational changes, its overall (perhaps unintended) effect was to leave the Scottish Conservatives with a confused leadership structure and a party organisation that was still directed towards a primary goal of power at Westminster. Strathclyde's organisational plan placed the Scottish Parliament firmly as a secondary concern. This structure remained in place until 2011. However, the Strathclyde reforms did begin to reverse some of the integration with the UK Conservative Party initiated under Margaret Thatcher in opposition in the 1970s (Stewart, 2009: 26).

In its interim report published on 13 December 1997, the Strathclyde Commission recommended that the party be joined together in a single unified structure. This was one of the most significant organisational changes. Thus, the previously separate professional, voluntary and parliamentary wings of the party should be united under an elected Chairman and an appointed Convenor. Management of the party would be split between a Scottish Executive and a Management Committee. However, in response to members' concerns (expressed during specially convened Strathclyde 'road-shows') about unclear lines of accountability under a 'two-headed monster' (Strathclyde Commission, 1998: 4), the final report published in 1998 revised this structure. Instead, there would be a single Scottish Executive running the party, with a Chairman appointed jointly by the Executive and the UK party leader and a Deputy Chairman elected by Scottish party members.

The report notes considerable discussion about the exact roles of Chairman and Deputy Chairman. For instance, we learn that 'the Commissioners have wrestled to find the right solution that would provide a direct chain of command, give a clear role to the national [UK] Leader of the party *and* produce a Chairman that would always be acceptable to members in Scotland' (Strathclyde Commission, 1998: 4). Moreover, although many members of the party thought that the way forward was to have an *elected* Chairman, others doubted this would work and could possibly deny the job to someone who had a career outside politics (Strathclyde Commission, 1998: 4). Crucially, the report is concerned with ensuring that the Chairman is 'safe in the knowledge that he had the ear of the [UK] Leader *and* the support of the party' (Strathclyde Commission, 1998: 5). The elected Deputy Chairman will sit on the UK party management board. Thus the report prioritises privileged access to the centre over a more distinctive form of Scottish leadership of the party.

One of the most striking aspects of the Strathclyde report is the status it accords the 'leader of the MSP group'. After the above detailed discussion about the exact constitutional status of the Chairman and Deputy Chairman, this position is mentioned for the first time on page 9. It lists the membership of the new Scottish Executive in the following order: Chairman, Deputy Chairman, Two Vice Chairmen, Members Elected at Conference, UK Parliament Representative, Member of the European Parliament, Leader of the MSPs. This position thus comes just after the MEP and just before the representative of Scottish Conservatives in Local Government and the Younger Members' Representative. In case the status of this position was not clear, the new constitution proposed by Strathclyde states at 9.2.16 that the MSPs' Leader is an *ex officio* member of the Scottish Executive.

The whole thrust of the Strathclyde Commission report is to maintain a highly integrated party where holding power at the UK level remains the priority. For any UK Conservative in 1998, the idea that the leader of the UK Conservative Party would not be in the House of Commons as a potential candidate to be prime minister would be regarded as absurd. Yet this is not how the commissioners, or most of the 1998 Scottish Conservative Party, viewed the Scottish Parliament or the chance of holding power in it. It was emphatically not the intention of the Strathclyde Commission to create a markedly separate party in Scotland. Instead, it sought to streamline an unwieldy Scottish party structure and slot the Scottish Parliament into it. A representative from the Scottish Parliament in the form of the Leader of the MSP Group would therefore feed into discussions about wider UK issues. The report is so wary of the consequences of further autonomy that it dare not even entertain the possibility of appointing a Chairman who does not have the support of the UK party leader.

This is emphatically not a party that sees the Scottish Parliament as marking a shift in the UK's governing arrangements towards something more akin to decentralisation in Spain or Germany. The main levers that it wishes to control remain at Westminster. It wants to be governed by a UK government through a Conservative territorial secretary of state. It does not want a strong or separate leadership structure in Scotland because every time the Strathclyde report mentions 'Leader', it refers implicitly to the UK party leader. The result is a curious hybrid structure that acknowledges the existence of the Scottish Parliament, but cannot quite come to terms with the implications for party organisation.

Table 3.4 Organisational structure recommended by the Strathclyde Commission (1998)

UK Leader		
Scottish Executive		Scottish Central Office
Policy Forum	Scottish Council	Area Forums
	Scottish Conference	
Membership in Associations		Agents

Source: Strathclyde Commission (1998: 24).

The Strathclyde Commission report is an example of the interplay of forces that impact on party organisational change. The external shocks of devolution and electoral defeat clashed with deeply engrained instincts about the place of Scotland and the Scottish Conservative Party in the UK, as well as the 'institutional stickiness' of an old political party. From the perspective of the present, it is sometimes easy to forget that the Scottish Conservatives had just come out of *government*. They saw the route back to government through the prism of the UK, not the Scottish Parliament.

When the Strathclyde arrangements confronted the reality of the Scottish Parliament there occurred the blurring of accountability and the lack of clarity about who was in charge that it had specifically sought to avoid. The Strathclyde organisational plan created two rival centres of power: the party in the Scottish Parliament and the party in Central Office. The assumption that the Leader of the MSP Group would be subordinate to the Party Chairman did not long survive the transition to the Scottish Parliament. Inevitably, the media assumed that the leader of the MSP group was the leader of the Scottish Conservative Party. The Scottish Parliament became the main focus for discussion of Scottish political issues and very quickly the MSP group had to deal with the media and with party lines and positions on debates. Aside from campaigning and fundraising issues, the party in Parliament became the main hub of political activity. At best, this caused tension and confusion with a Chairman located in Central Office at the other side of Edinburgh; at worst it was source of dysfunction and disagreement.

For one party official working in Parliament:

> You had Central Office who believed that the MSPs were useless, that the staff who worked for the MSPs were all poisonous. And to a certain degree both of those statements were true. And you had people at the Parliament, principally the staff at the Parliament, who thought that Central Office were failures, were over-promoted, and, you know, to a certain degree that was true as well. (Interview with Scottish official 3, 10 October 2011)

Ultimately, the officials working in Central Office did not answer to anyone working in the Parliament. This was 'a symptom of a party who doesn't know who is boss' (interview with Scottish official 3, 10 October 2011). Similarly, another official comments:

> You still had the problem of who was in charge … you had Peter [Duncan], Shadow Scottish Secretary, the only Scottish MP, big job, big name, and then you had David McLetchie, leader of the group. Who is in charge? And that at the end of the day is a problem. (Interview with Scottish official 1, 25 October 2011)

One former leader attaches less significance to this but still noted that the situation was unsatisfactory: 'In some respects I found that it was a problem in the sense that you had an authority that was very much limited by reference to the fact that you were leader in the parliament as opposed to leader elsewhere and it might therefore have been a better situation if I had been overall leader' (interview with MSP 8, 2 October 2012). For another former leader, however:

> It was a problem. I mean, it wasn't a problem in the sense that I didn't get on with the people who had these responsibilities. I did get on with them. But it was a problem in the sense of, I felt at times, I had three horses, I was sitting in the driver's seat of the wagon, but I only had one set of reins in my hand. And while the other horses were roughly going in the same way, I really wanted at times to just take all the reins and say, we're going that way. And I couldn't do that. (Interview with MSP 9, 24 October 2012)

This confusion about responsibilities was compounded by the complicated arrangement of mandates for the different officials and politicians in charge. The Leader of the MSP Group was elected by an electoral college of 70 per cent MSPs and 30 per cent party members (Strathclyde Commission, 1998: 9); the Chairman was appointed by the Scottish Executive along with the UK party leader; and the Deputy Chairman was elected by party members (Strathclyde Commission, 1998: 8). As one party official explains, such an arrangement 'clearly gave that Deputy Chairman a position that was, you could argue, more one in tune with the membership than the political leader of the party. I think that was one that came back to haunt the party later on and caused some of the difficulties that ensued'.

The Scottish Conservatives thus felt quite acutely the distinction identified by Katz and Mair (1994) between the different 'faces' of a political party: the *party in public office* was often in conflict with the *party in central office*. Although such tensions between Central Office and politicians are certainly not unprecedented in the Conservative Party (see, for example, Kavanagh, 2005: 226; Bale, 2012: 167), here they were written into the very constitution of the party.

Sanderson Commission (2010)

The Sanderson Commission was established by the Scottish Conservatives in response to their poor showing at the 2010 UK general election. Lord Sanderson of Bowden (a former party chairman and Scottish Office minister) chaired a panel drawn from all sections of the party (including councillors and Lord Forsyth) to 'review the structures, function and operational activity of the Scottish Conservative and Unionist Party and to recommend any changes that would strengthen the Party as a modern, effective, political campaigning entity in Scotland'. It openly acknowledges from the outset that electoral results have been disappointing and that 'current confusion of roles and responsibilities contributes significantly to what is seen widely to be a lack of clarity of leadership, accountability and decision-making' (Sanderson Commission, 2010: 10). Thus, the main thrust of the Commission's recommendations was to streamline the structure of the Scottish Conservatives and place in charge a leader elected by the membership. It also recommended a rationalisation of the party's regional structures and more professional staff. Nevertheless, it is still possible to detect the tensions in the Conservative Party's unionist thought throughout the report. Whilst this is a clear example of party organisational change, the Sanderson Commission also reflects the split between 'devolutionists' and 'assimilationists' that would later emerge in the open during the 2011 leadership election.

The recommendation that there be a clear leader of the party elected by the membership tidied up one of the legacies of the Strathclyde Commission (Sanderson Commission, 2010: 16). Yet still the Sanderson Commission felt the need to ensure that the leader need not be an MSP (Sanderson Commission, 2010: 16). This again injects into the organisational structure of the Scottish Conservatives a lack of seriousness about holding power in the Scottish Parliament. Would a deputy first minister in a coalition Conservative administration be taken seriously if he or she was not the leader of the party but instead nominally answered to another party activist who might be an MP or a councillor? Again, any UK Conservative would be highly unlikely ever to contemplate such a structure.

The report is also concerned to protect the Scottish Conservatives' access to the UK centre. In rejecting the need for an entirely separate party in Scotland, it notes, first, that the 'Scottish Conservatives obtain numerous benefits from being part of the UK Party, including the opportunity to access resources, training and expertise and for members to vote for the UK leader' (Sanderson Commission, 2010: 14). Second, it states that the UK party benefits from the input of the Scottish party on policy development. Such a structure, it argues, is entirely fitting with the Scottish Conservatives' desire to retain the Union. Third, and most practically, it rejects a 'CDU/CSU' arrangement on the basis that the CSU is the dominant party in Bavarian politics and is therefore able to fund itself. Referring implicitly to the subsidy the Scottish Conservatives receive from the English party, it concludes: 'Scottish Conservatives have greater advantages to gain from being both autonomous and part of the UK Conservative Party' (Sanderson Commission, 2010: 14).

The Commission also recommends a much simpler central management structure for the party. The Scottish Leader is unambiguously in charge and sits on a management board alongside the Chairman, three new regional convenors, the party treasurer and the party director. The three regional convenors (voluntary party members) are to work alongside three full-time regional campaign managers, employed centrally by the party. Underneath the overarching Management Board sits a Fundraising and Finance Board, a Political Strategy Group (with representatives from the MEP group, Westminster and councillors), a Candidates Board, three Regional Councils and a Scottish Convention (the equivalent of the annual party conference).

In addition to the new full-time regional campaign managers, the Sanderson Commission recommends the appointment of a Chief Policy Adviser (Sanderson Commission, 2010: 26). In this vein, it also laments the Scottish Conservatives' lack of engagement with think-tanks (particularly the centre-right Reform Scotland) and even with its own members about formulation of policy. There should be much more consultation with members, twice yearly 'policy conferences' and substantive motions to be debated at the party's annual conference.

The Sanderson recommendations were on the whole adopted at a special conference. There were some changes to procedures for selecting candidates. However, although this is a clear manifestation of internal party organisational change that attempts to deal with the reality of devolution, it does not guarantee wider acceptance of a Conservative vision for the Scottish Parliament. The *formal* organisation of a party may be different from its *enacted* organisation.

Territorial organisational autonomy

The Scottish Conservative Party is a territorial branch of the UK Conservative Party. It therefore faces all of the challenges associated with being a statewide party in a regional context. However, the prevailing attitudes of elites within the UK Conservative Party and the structure of the devolution arrangements resulted in the Scottish Conservatives having a high degree of autonomy (Convery, 2014a). This section examines the autonomy of the Scottish Conservative Party over the central areas of leadership selection, candidate selection, policy-making and finance (Laffin et al., 2007).

Leadership selection

The post-devolution Conservatives have had only one leadership election. David McLetchie was elected in 1999 at a specially convened selection meeting of party grandees and candidates and Annabel Goldie was elected unopposed in 2005. The process for the leadership election in 2011 was devised in Scotland under the Sanderson Commission and whilst there were some rumours that David Cameron backed Ruth Davidson, the leadership election was free from central control. Even had the UK Conservative Party wanted to intervene, it could only have done so to a limited extent in terms of providing tacit endorsements or advice. The Sanderson Commission (2010) rules mean that the leader is selected only by members of the Scottish party on a one-member-one-vote basis using the alternative vote electoral system.

Candidate selection

The area of candidate selection still bears the legacy of the previously separate Scottish Conservative Party and the importance of constituency associations in the wider Conservative Party. Central Office in London did not generally interfere with candidate selection for Westminster. Before the first Scottish Parliament elections, a similarly separate system was put in place. Candidate selection is the sole responsibility of the Scottish party. Unlike the Labour Party, for example, there have been no high-profile examples of interference from London in selection of candidates for the devolved legislature.

However, in the case of by-elections for Westminster during Cameron's leadership, UK Central Office took a much greater interest. This has led to candidates being put in place from outside constituency associations. Yet it would be a mistake to view this as the UK Central Office trampling on an association's autonomy. In the case of Ruth Davidson in the Glasgow North East by-election in 2009, for example, the party was pleased to have a candidate with such a high profile. By-elections for Westminster seats were not contentious because the Scottish Conservative Party was not at this stage in danger of winning any of them.

Policy-making

Like many European parties on the moderate centre-right, the Conservative Party is a highly centralised organisation when it comes to making policy. Bale (2012) examines frequent instances of initiatives to involve party members in the making of policy, but finds little evidence that policies adopted are marked by the influence of the various formal committees and structures put in place to gather the views of members. This is also the case in the Scottish Conservative Party where the party at large has little role in the final drafting of the manifesto. For instance, the party took a pick and mix approach to the recommendations of an arm's length policy group of party members and non-members set up before the 2007 Holyrood elections (Torrance, 2012: 104). For the 2007 manifesto, one MSP concluded that 'ultimately, the policy was decided effectively by the leader and a small team who took the final decisions' (interview with MSP 1, 6 March 2012).

All of the MSPs interviewed by the author confirmed that the Scottish Conservatives had almost complete policy autonomy on all of the areas under the Scottish Parliament's control. One MSP cannot recall any instances of clashes:

> I think the autonomy is actually pretty good. Throughout William Hague's period of leadership, IDS, Howard ... I mean basically, they cut us a lot of slack and we could actually move on quite a number of these areas, so I think the autonomy aspect of it worked pretty well and we didn't have any major issues with that ... I think probably the most sensitive area in that regard would be in relation to fishing, although we did sort of try and push the boat out in that regard. But otherwise actually I found with William and IDS and then Michael Howard, I mean I actually found quite a lot of slack there, to be honest. (Interview with MSP 8, 2 October 2012)

Similarly, asked if there were any 'no-go' areas in terms of devolved policy-making, another MSP comments:

> No. Absolutely not. And in fact, to be fair, and credit must be paid initially to William Hague because he said ... at that time, look, you know, devolved Parliament, Scotland Act, you've got powers, you now deal with issues that have nothing to do with Westminster, you are absolutely in control over policy-making. And that was reaffirmed by Iain Duncan Smith, Michael Howard and David Cameron. And there were

things where I did things slightly differently in devolved policy. Perhaps notably in our justice portfolio we took a slightly different approach to things. We also ... we were interestingly in the vanguard with our drugs policy. I mean Iain Duncan Smith was very interested in what we were doing up here, and when we got that new drugs strategy delivered, which was a Conservative policy, you know, down south were very interested in that. So in a sense we kind of led in some areas, never mind diverged. So, no, I never felt constrained and I know Ruth doesn't either. (Interview with MSP 9, 24 October 2012)

This attitude of benign neglect or pragmatism at the UK level fits with wider considerations of what might be the priorities of elites at the top of the Conservative Party (see, for instance, Bulpitt, 1983, 1986; Convery, 2014a). It also chimes with some of what is known about attitudes towards the Scottish Conservatives in the UK Conservative Party. Writing about the 1950s Conservative Party, Bale (2012: 62) notes that the 'party north of the border continued to be a standing joke in London until well into the next century' (see also Bale, 2012: 77, 192–193).

Finance

During the early years of the Scottish Parliament, the Conservatives in Scotland were able to rely on donations from Lord Laidlaw. However, he ceased to donate to the party after the 2010 general election. In exchange for providing the money to support the implementation of the Sanderson reforms, the Scottish party agreed that all money raised in Scotland should go through Conservative Campaign Headquarters (CCHQ) in London. A proportion is then returned to Scotland to spend each year. However, one senior party official still insists that the Scottish Conservatives can raise enough money to cover their costs and that the new arrangement with the UK party simply gives financial security (interview with Scottish official 4, 30 November 2012). Whether the Scottish Conservatives would have enough money to survive if they broke away from the UK Conservative Party was a key debate during the 2011 leadership election (Convery, 2014b).

Personnel

The Scottish Conservatives still bear the mark of the initial candidate selection procedures and the candidates adopted to stand at the first Scottish Parliament elections in 1999. Elected members are the public face of a political party and drive its everyday campaigning and policy agenda. This is particularly the case in a political party like the Conservatives in which so much power (especially in opposition) is placed in the hands of a leadership drawn from its ranks of elected politicians. However, aside from the election in 2011 of the openly gay Ruth Davidson, there have been no major personnel changes that can be said to have represented significant party change.

Table 3.5 Conservative Members of the Scottish Parliament, 1999–2011

Constituency

	1999	2003	2007	2011
Ayr		John Scott	John Scott	John Scott
Edinburgh Pentlands		David McLetchie	David McLetchie	
Galloway and Upper Nithsdale		Alex Fergusson	Alex Fergusson	Alex Fergusson
Roxburgh and Berwickshire			John Lamont	John Lamont

Regional list

	1999	2003	2007	2011
Central Scotland	Lyndsay McIntosh	Margaret Mitchell	Margaret Mitchell	Margaret Mitchell
Glasgow	Bill Aitken	Bill Aitken	Bill Aitken	Ruth Davidson
Highlands and Islands	Jamie MacGrigor Mary Scanlon	Jamie MacGrigor Mary Scanlon	Jamie MacGrigor Mary Scanlon	Jamie MacGrigor Mary Scanlon
Lothian	James Douglas-Hamilton David McLetchie	James Douglas-Hamilton	Gavin Brown	David McLetchie Gavin Brown
Mid-Scotland and Fife	Keith Harding Nick Johnstone Brian Monteith	Ted Brocklebank Murdo Fraser Brian Monteith	Ted Brocklebank Murdo Fraser Elizabeth Smith	Murdo Fraser Elizabeth Smith
North East Scotland	David Davidson Alex Johnstone Ben Wallace	David Davidson Alex Johnstone Nanette Milne	Alex Johnstone Nanette Milne	Alex Johnstone Nanette Milne
South Scotland	Alex Fergusson Phil Gallie David Mundell Murray Tosh	Phil Gallie David Mundell	Derek Brownlee	
West Scotland	Annabel Goldie John Young	Annabel Goldie Murray Tosh	Annabel Goldie Jackson Carlaw	Annabel Goldie Jackson Carlaw

Source: Scottish Parliament (2013).

Policy

One of the most important ways in which a political party can demonstrate change is through its policy platform, particularly as outlined in a manifesto. Dropping once cherished but now unpopular policies in order to change a party's image, for instance, is a clear sign of party change. However, the policy process in political parties is subject to the same path dependent processes as its organisation. As Bale (2012: 149) points out, 'a policy is more likely to be included in a party's offer to the electorate if it is dreamt up earlier, rather than later in the process'. Similarly, in the absence of new ideas, parties may reach for ideas which have been tried before and which are known to fit with members' or (perceived) supporters' views or the party's sense of ideology. The Scottish Conservative Party lost its once formidable indigenous capacity for producing Tory policies specifically for Scotland. For most of the Conservative governments (1979–1997) the party concentrated instead on tailoring English policies for a Scottish context, a process one party official labels as 'tartanisation' (interview with Scottish official 2, 2 November 2011).

Similarly, in the post-devolution period, the party struggled both to adjust to the prevailing policy mood in Scotland and to come up with original ideas that addressed the central issues over which the Scottish Parliament has competence in a manner that did not appear out of date or extreme. Thus, the party's policy platform can only be said to have changed in quite limited ways since 1997. In particular, in the key Scottish Parliament areas of health and education, the party in 2011 (and in many respects in 2015) was essentially repackaging the type of reforms that it had pursued in government in Scotland (1979–1997). The most significant policy change for the Scottish Conservatives occurred as a result of the second Strathclyde Commission's proposals for further devolution in light of the 2014 referendum.

This section considers firstly the policy-making of the Scottish Conservative Party in the pre-devolution era. It then examines the main post-1997 report on Scottish Conservative policy, *Scotland's Future*, written under the chairmanship of Sir Malcolm Rifkind. Finally, it considers the post-devolution policies of the Scottish Conservative Party. Devolution has had a limited impact on the party's policies beyond further powers for the Scottish Parliament.

The making of pre-devolution Scottish Conservative Party policy

There is a distinguished tradition of Conservative Party policy that is made in Scotland for Scotland. The loss of this strand of thinking capacity was a major contributor to the decline of the Conservatives in Scotland (Stewart, 2009). Scottish Conservative MPs have also had a major influence on aspects of the philosophy of the UK Conservative Party (see, for instance, Torrance (2010) on Noel Skelton and the idea of a 'property-owning democracy'). Moreover, 'the Conservative Party more than any other in the 20th century contributed to the development of the distinct Scottish politics which was mobilised by supporters of a Scottish Parliament'

(Mitchell and Convery, 2012: 170). Not only did the Conservatives create the Scottish Office; they oversaw its expansion and development well into the 1990s. The preservation of the distinctiveness of Scottish political and economic institutions from the dangers of excessive centralisation and anglification was once a central part of its message. For instance, Scottish Unionists campaigned against the new organisations created by the Attlee Government to run the new nationalised industries in Scotland, arguing that separate Scottish boards should be created (Mitchell, 1990: 27). The 1949 Scottish Unionists were the type of party that could produce a document entitled *Scottish Control of Scottish Affairs*, which recommended further strengthening the role of the Scottish Office and of Scottish oversight of nationalised industries (Scottish Unionist Party, 1949; Bale, 2012: 32).

It would be overstating matters to paint a picture of a golden age of Scottish Conservative policy-making. Nevertheless, it is clear that whatever post-war capacity existed gradually declined and increasingly the Scottish Conservatives looked to the centre to provide a lead. Particularly in the 1980s, the Scottish Conservatives sought to either refashion English Conservative policies for a Scottish context (Stewart, 2009: 45) or, even more reactively, adopt a strategy of being seen to protect Scotland from the harsher edges of UK Conservative policies (Mitchell, 1990: 98–99; Torrance, 2009: 45).

A Scottish Conservative official summarises the thinking of the pre-devolution Scottish Conservatives like this:

> The strategy, I suppose, was to try and make Thatcherism work in Scotland. We were still trying to sell, sort of traditional, the safe message that we were selling across the UK, but at the same time we were trying to develop, I suppose, more of a Scottish identity ... but the policies were by and large Scottish versions of what was happening across the UK. There wasn't that much deviation, despite the fact there was a Scottish Office.

Being in government meant that the Scottish Office remained central to the policy-making machinery for the party:

> I mean, I was a fairly junior researcher at the time. But yes a lot of our policy came from the special advisers at the Scottish Office. It would come down to us and we would relay it to the wider party ... there was more policy because we were in government so we had to make policy on everything pretty much. So, yes, it would have been set at a UK level absolutely. The short answer is that there wasn't a Scottish element to that. We were 'Scottifying' policies.

In such a context, therefore:

> there wasn't seen to be a need for a Scottish identity in the party, and in policy in particular, and therefore it was just tartan versions of what was happening down south. You know, there was still a belief that we could sell a united, unionist message across the UK and you didn't have to have different policies in Scotland to those in the rest of the UK. And that was very much where we were coming from. We weren't really

arguing for a sort of, any sort of decentralising perspective. That wasn't the way it worked. It was, you know, devolution, no, Thatcherism, yes. That was the slogan at the time. We didn't want devolution. What we wanted was a more Conservative, with a capital 'C', message ... tooth and claw if you like. We would be blue. (Interview with Scottish official 2, 2 November 2011)

Such an analysis is supported by consideration of the 1992 Scottish Conservative manifesto. John Major's flagship public services policy, the *Citizen's Charter*, is revised for a Scottish context (Scottish Conservative Party, 1992: 14). In education, the parental choice agenda is central: schools should publish performance data so that parents can make decisions. The assisted places scheme (through which the state pays for poor children to go to private schools) is to be maintained (Scottish Conservative Party, 1992: 18). Apart from the inheritance of the distinctive Scottish curriculum and examinations system, these policies do not in any significant way deviate from the broad thrust of English Conservative education policy. Similarly, in the NHS, GP fundholding is to be extended in Scotland (Scottish Conservative Party, 1992: 30). At best, Scottish Conservatives did not so much lose the ability to think for themselves as decide that the best way forward for the country was for such thinking to be carried out at the UK level and adapted for Scotland.

The Rifkind policy commission

Alongside the Strathclyde organisational reforms, the Scottish Conservatives also asked Sir Malcolm Rifkind (who had just lost his Edinburgh Pentlands seat) to chair a policy commission to look at a post-devolution direction for the party. The resulting *Scotland's Future* report is a document which serves as an eclectic menu of options, rather than a coherent way forward (Scottish Conservative Party, 1998). It covers everything from raising teachers' salaries (p.18) to the importance of having live arrivals information at bus stops for passengers' peace of mind (p.52). Nevertheless, there are flashes of ideas that might begin to move towards a new agenda. Interestingly, it proposes some quite radical constitutional innovations that were never subsequently taken up. It recommends that a Royal Commission on the House of Lords should consider whether the House should have a regional representative structure similar to the German Bundesrat (Scottish Conservative Party, 1998: 6). The Westminster Parliament should also give a 'binding commitment that devolution legislation could never be abrogated without the consent of the Scottish Parliament' (Scottish Conservative Party, 1998: 6). The report also suggests that Scotland deserves a 'premier' not a 'first minister' and a 'government' not an 'executive', a change introduced by the SNP government in 2007.

However, this report also marks the first point at which we can detect that the pre-1997 policy agenda will be difficult for the Conservatives to shake off. The Commission, as it insists, probably did not feel 'any need to ensure that our recommendations are consistent with Conservative policy in England and Wales' and doubtless intended to have 'clear differences in ... approach with those south of the border' (Scottish Conservative Party, 1998: 5). Nevertheless, apart from something reasonably distinctive on fishing (p.43), the report stays in the main within the parameters set by the previous 18 years of Conservative policy towards Scotland.

Thus, once again, power is to be devolved directly to teachers from local authorities so that they are in total charge of their school (Scottish Conservative Party, 1998: 18; also proposed in Scottish Conservative Party, 1992: 18; Scottish Conservative Party, 1999: 10; Scottish Conservative Party, 2003: 16). Moreover, not content with the measure of parental choice they have already injected into the system, the Rifkind Commission proposes a longer-term investigation into a school voucher system (along the same lines as the parents' and patients' passports explored under Iain Duncan Smith – see Bale, 2010: 147) which could be used at state or private schools and topped up by parents (Scottish Conservative Party, 1998: 19). Considering the fact that only two of Scotland's 2,500 schools took up the opportunity provided by the Conservatives to become 'grant-maintained' outside local authority control in the 1990s (McKenzie, 2001: 95), it seems odd that the Conservatives would attempt to continue along this path. Taken to its logical conclusion, even if the Conservatives won a majority in the new Scottish Parliament and were in a position to introduce such a system, it is not at all clear that the Scottish educational establishment would co-operate in its implementation. Considerable political capital would have to be spent on battling opposition to what would be described as the further 'marketisation' and even 'privatisation' of the education system. Taking on professional vested interests may be considered a noble Conservative cause in a Scottish political system otherwise dominated by the centre-left, but here the Conservatives appear to have badly misread the extent of the 'zone of acquiescence' in education policy.[4]

Similarly, recommendations on the NHS show the limited extent of new thinking and also bear the mark of UK Conservative policies. GP fundholding and the NHS internal market should be maintained (Scottish Conservative Party, 1998: 14), in addition to the perennial favourite of bringing back matron (Scottish Conservative Party, 1998: 15).

Overall, it is perhaps being too harsh on the Scottish Conservatives to expect them within a year of the 1997 electoral disaster to come up with a fresh and exciting policy agenda. In the UK context, such new thinking was also absent (Bale, 2010), although there were stirrings about the extent to which the Conservatives would have to change in order to regain power.

Post-devolution Scottish Conservative Party policy-making

The policy positions of the Scottish Conservative Party show little evidence of significant party change outside the field of further devolution. Indeed, it is arguable that the intellectual foundations for their policies are still those that informed the writing of the 1992 manifesto. Devolution has not provided a sufficient shock to its attitudes to engender a radical rethinking of policies for implementation in a Scottish context. This has at times prevented the Scottish Conservatives from engaging constructively in debates about the future of, for instance, Scottish public services.

1999 manifesto

The first manifesto for the 1999 Scottish Parliament elections explicitly acknowledges such a danger. David McLetchie's foreword concedes that people thought that 'our decisions and policies had London stamped all over them, with little relevance, or sympathy, for the needs of the Scottish people' (Scottish Conservative Party, 1999: 1). The manifesto also begins with a strong commitment to the success of the Scottish Parliament, suggesting that the civil service should be spread throughout Scotland (Scottish Conservative Party, 1999: 3). Nevertheless, the rest of the manifesto does not represent a significant step forward from previous policies. It has a firm commitment to a low tax economy (Scottish Conservative Party, 1999: 5) and to removing 'red tape' (Scottish Conservative Party, 1999: 7). It proposes giving parents 'vouchers' worth the equivalent of a full year's nursery education place for a four-year-old which they can spend wherever they want (Scottish Conservative Party, 1999: 10). Again, education is to be taken out of the hands of local authorities; instead it should be invested in 'school boards' bringing together groups of schools which each have greater freedom (Scottish Conservative Party, 1999: 10).

Similarly, in health the Scottish Conservatives propose taking powers away from health boards and returning to GP fundholding (Scottish Conservative Party, 1999: 14). In addition, its seven key pledges include lifting the beef-on-the-bone ban, abolishing university tuition fees and introducing 'modern matrons' into hospitals (Scottish Conservative Party, 1999: 2). Its positions are based around responses to statements about what Labour has done in government (increased taxes or regulation) and has photographs of voters asking questions like: 'Why wasn't I told about the new taxes?' (Scottish Conservative Party, 1999: 5).

2003 manifesto

The 2003 manifesto marks something of a step backward in terms of presenting a positive image of devolution. On almost the opening page it has a big picture of a mock Hollywood sign which reads 'Follyrood' (Scottish Conservative Party, 2003: 3). It then goes on to propose cutting the number of MSPs to 108 by making constituency MSPs operate on the new smaller number of Westminster seats (Scottish Conservative Party, 2003: 5). In an early sign of unease about the powers of the Scottish Parliament, it proposes a Royal Commission to examine its future.

Zero-tolerance policing is again a key feature, alongside the conviction that 'prison works' (Scottish Conservative Party, 2003: 7–8). On the NHS, the Scottish Conservatives indicate once again that they are against the NHS public sector monopoly, although they pledge to stick to current NHS spending plans (Scottish

Conservative Party, 2003: 11). Once again, GP fundholding is to be restored, alongside an internal market in which 'money follows the patient' (Scottish Conservative Party, 2003: 12). In education, parental choice remains central to the Conservatives' plans. More power should be devolved away from local authorities and towards head teachers. An early version of Michael Gove's free schools policy is also proposed (Scottish Conservative Party, 2003: 16).

2007 manifesto

In 2007, as in 2003, we again see a theme of disappointment with devolution (Scottish Conservative Party, 2007: 2). There is also a quiet acknowledgement that the fiscal powers of the Scottish Parliament are problematic (Scottish Conservative Party, 2007: 17). In education, again more power is to be devolved to head teachers, but some role for local authorities is still envisaged (Scottish Conservative Party, 2007: 26). Free schools have gone, but the manifesto suggests a pilot of one city academy in Glasgow (Scottish Conservative Party, 2007: 28). The tuition fees pledge is dropped and instead a commission will examine the future funding of higher education (Scottish Conservative Party, 2007: 28).

2007–2011: policy relevance for the Scottish Conservatives

By supporting the budgets of the minority SNP Government (2007–2011), the Scottish Conservative Party was able to negotiate policy concessions. During this time, it claims to have achieved: 1,000 extra police officers; a four-year council tax freeze; cuts in business rates; a new drugs strategy; a town centre regeneration fund; and a £26 million investment in housing (Scottish Conservative Party, 2011: 1). Thus, the Conservatives during this period were adept at being an opposition party in a multi-party parliament (interview with MSP 6, 8 May 2012). In particular, the party's finance spokesman, Derek Brownlee, developed a good working relationship with the SNP's Finance Secretary, John Swinney. Derek Brownlee also hoped that voting with the SNP would help detoxify the party's brand and bring it back into the mainstream of Scottish politics (Torrance, 2012: 107). However, the co-operative working with the SNP had a limited impact on changing the Scottish Conservatives.

2011 manifesto

The 2011 manifesto takes as its theme 'Common Sense for Scotland'. This has echoes of William Hague's leadership of the UK party (1997–2001) when he proposed a 'Common Sense Revolution' (Hayton, 2012: 49). Across the public services, the party proposes to abolish the SNP's concordat with Scottish councils; pilot social impact bonds; and follow the UK Conservative Party by requiring local authorities to make public items of expenditure over £500 (Scottish Conservative Party, 2011: 9–10). In 2011, education policy draws on the Rifkind Commission to

Table 3.6 The evolution of Scottish Conservative policy on key public services

	1999	2003	2007	2011
Education	More power to head teachers; parental choice	More power to head teachers; parental choice	More power to head teachers; parental choice; pilot of one city academy in Glasgow	Parental choice through school vouchers; free schools
Health	Return to GP fundholding	Return to GP fundholding	Money follows patient through the system (patients' decisions informed by GPs)	Review of the Scottish NHS structure

Source: Scottish Conservative Party (1999, 2003, 2007, 2011).

propose school vouchers equal to the value of a year's education in the state sector that can be spent with any provider (Scottish Conservative Party, 2011: 12). In higher education in 2011, the Scottish Conservatives were the only party to propose introducing a graduate contribution to university fees (Scottish Conservative Party, 2011: 14).

In health, the Scottish Conservatives propose to protect the NHS budget and establish a cancer drugs fund. The commitment to an NHS internal market is dropped and replaced with a proposal to review the structure of the Scottish NHS (Scottish Conservative Party, 2011: 16–17).

Overall, policy change in the post-devolution Scottish Conservative Party has been limited and incremental. It is to a large extent still informed by the party's experience in government in Scotland. In 2013, Ruth Davidson again proposed school vouchers in her speech to the Scottish Conservative Party conference.

The referendum and the second Strathclyde Commission

However, beyond the public policy under the control of the Scottish Parliament, the Scottish Conservatives have managed under Ruth Davidson to significantly alter their stance on the issue of the future of the United Kingdom. Davidson commissioned Lord Strathclyde to write a report on what further devolution the Conservatives should adopt in the event that Scots voted to remain in the UK. The proposals of the Strathclyde Commission (Scottish Conservative Party, 2014) were accepted by the party in full in a manner that suggested the splits of the 2011 leadership election over devolution were resolved in favour of more powers. Although the former Scottish Secretary Lord Forsyth predictably denounced the proposals (*The Scotsman*, 2014), the closeness of the referendum campaign and the result cemented the idea in the party that the union was in danger from a lack of a compelling alternative. When fully 45 per cent of the electorate votes for independence (a prospect that is utterly inimical to everything the Scottish Conservative Party stands for, however ineffectively), it becomes much harder to sustain the argument that the union is best protected by maintaining the status quo.

Crucially, the Commission report attempted to reconcile unionism and conservatism:

> When these actions are taken within the context of Conservative policies on empowering individuals and decentralising power throughout the rest of the UK, it is clear that empowering the Scottish people to shape their own nation within the security of a United Kingdom is not just something we are willing only grudgingly to accept, it is something that sits at the very heart of what it means to be a modern Scottish Conservative. (Scottish Conservative Party, 2014: 3–4)

The report is therefore significant in two central ways. First, it took the Conservative Party 15 years to arrive at this conclusion about further powers for the Scottish Parliament. Instead of viewing every new power for the Scottish Parliament as a concession to the Scottish National Party, the Conservatives now had a Conservative statement about the centre-right case for further (particularly fiscal) autonomy. Second, by pushing the debate beyond the Calman Commission, this marked the first time since the 1960s that the Scottish Conservatives had their own unique offer on devolution. Significantly, in proposing the devolution of all income tax rates and bands to the Scottish Parliament, the Strathclyde proposals outflanked the Labour Party's, resulting in the Conservatives having the most ambitious statewide party policy on further powers apart from the Liberal Democrats. It was armed for the first time since devolution with an ideologically coherent position on further powers.

Conclusion

For the Scottish Conservative Party, the introduction of devolution was a traumatic experience. Not only did it come after a crushing defeat for the party in 1997, it also struck at the heart of its conception of unionism. The Scottish Conservatives undoubtedly embraced devolution at a practical level, participating fully in the Parliament, providing one of their number to be presiding officer, and even during 2007–2011 becoming a significant and relevant opposition party. Pragmatic Conservatives could hardly do otherwise when faced with a new governing institution. However, this level of engagement was superficial. The Conservatives never managed (at least until 2014) to absorb the Scottish Parliament at a philosophical level.

In policy terms, they found it difficult to grasp that many of the policies they pursued in the 1980s and 1990s in Scotland would never have been considered, far less implemented, had it not been for the peculiar structure of the British state, under which the colour of territorial governments was decided by electoral politics at the UK level. There is an extent to which the Scottish Conservatives towards the end of the twentieth century were artificially sustained in a set of policies and attitudes that went beyond their mandate. Acknowledging this, and then trying to place themselves and their policies on the centre-right of a *Scottish* (as opposed to British) political spectrum, was a step the Scottish Conservatives could never quite take. They became dependent on a stock of answers which served them well in the 1980s and 1990s, but which were viewed in post-devolution Scotland as at best old-fashioned and at worst extreme or even English. Until the 2011 leadership election, the Scottish Conservatives never seriously considered breaking out of this inheritance. However, in that election, they opted for cosmetic rather than radical change by electing Ruth Davidson over Murdo Fraser.

The most significant changes in the post-devolution Scottish Conservative Party concerned organisation. The electoral defeats of 1997 and 2010 prompted the party to appoint commissions to consider the future. Although devolution was a factor in driving these changes, on balance it is fair to say that electoral defeat was a more potent spur for change in a party that still set so much store by the priority of Westminster office.

The autonomy of the Scottish Conservatives did not change over the post-devolution period. The UK Conservative Party adopted a policy of benign neglect towards its territorial branches, leaving the Scottish Conservatives in particular with complete autonomy over policy and candidate and leadership selection. There were not substantial changes in party personnel over this period.

Broadly, two paths faced the Scottish Conservatives in 1999: embrace or tolerate devolution. In the end, they chose to follow neither. Instead, they sought a middle road which avoided party conflict, wholeheartedly embraced the Parliament at a procedural level, and left them after 2007 being compared unfavourably to their Welsh colleagues whose attitude and election results suggested they might be dealing rather better with the regional/national dilemma.

Notes

1 A fuller history of the early Tory Party in Scotland is given in Warner (1988). On party organisation in the twentieth century, see Urwin (1965) and Ward (1982).
2 For instance, Teddy Taylor's election leaflet in 1964 in Glasgow Cathcart does not mention the Conservative Party at all and instead talks about the need for a 'Unionist Government' (Taylor, 2008: 83–84).
3 The perceived existence of these 'missing Conservatives' was also apparent after 1997 in the UK Conservative Party. Some MPs thought they could be brought back

if the party moved to the right on certain issues (Snowdon, 2010: 42; see also Bale, 2010: 72).
4 However, it should be noted that (outside the limitations of Scottish political debate) school choice is not necessarily inimical to the progressive ends that all of the Scottish political parties claim to support. See, for instance, Paterson (2007) or Le Grand (2007).

4

Devolution, party change and the Welsh Conservative Party

We have parked our tanks on the nationalists' lawns in a sense. (Interview with Conservative AM 3, 1 March 2012)

Introduction

This chapter applies the analytical framework outlined in Chapter 2 to the Welsh Conservative Party. It finds that the Welsh Conservatives faced similar challenges to the Scottish Conservatives in adapting to devolution. It is arguable that initially the Scottish Conservatives adapted much better to the transition from the referendum to the new institutions. However, the election of Nick Bourne as leader of the party became a key driver for party change at the elite level in the Welsh Conservatives. In particular, he encouraged a new attitude towards the party's policies and image which was much more supportive of Welsh aspirations. This did not represent a wholesale conversion of the party to devolution (particularly at the level of the party membership), but it did ensure that at the elite level the party was able to manoeuvre itself into a position where it was on the cusp of coalition government in 2007 with Plaid Cymru and the Liberal Democrats. Thus, whilst it is easy for some in the Scottish party to exaggerate the extent of the party change which occurred in the Welsh Conservatives, it is clear that there has been much more change than in Scotland.

Unlike the Scottish Conservative Party, the Welsh Conservative Party started out with less formal autonomy in 1997 and did not gain any more over the course of its separate existence. Instead, it pushed at the limits of its autonomy and found that the central party did not object (Convery, 2014a). For the Welsh Conservatives, the lack of clearly defined party structures presented fewer powerful actors to consult and fewer forums for dissent from the leadership's strategy. The party was, in Panebianco's (1988: 261) terms, less institutionalised than in Scotland and this resulted in fewer obstacles to change. In short, the main driver of party change was a group of people who thought autonomously, rather than formal structures that granted autonomy. Such changes were also aided by a much more clearly defined intellectual project of renewal in Welsh Conservatism (akin to the movement which provided the foundations for the Cameron agenda), outlined by figures such as Jonathan Evans and David Melding, and enthusiastically (but subtly) adopted under Bourne's leadership.

This chapter begins by examining the history of the Welsh Conservative Party and in particular the party's attitudes towards Wales during the Conservative Governments (1979–1997). It then considers the evolution of devolution in Wales. The widely perceived inadequacies of the powers and structure of the Welsh Assembly provided a key opportunity for the Conservatives to engage with the devolution project. This chapter then examines the potential drivers of party change for the Welsh Conservatives and finds leadership change to be the most significant. Finally, this chapter analyses the manifestations of party change in Wales. Whilst there has been little organisational change, the policies and the image the party has tried to project have changed significantly.

History of the Welsh Conservative Party

Unlike the Scottish Conservative Party, the Welsh Conservatives have no history of a distinctly separate organisational or political identity. Similarly, the sense of Welsh political nationhood was much less developed than in Scotland in 1997. With some notable exceptions, especially on measures to protect and enhance the Welsh language, the Conservative Party dealt with Wales largely as it would have an English local authority (Melding, 2009: 124). Such an inheritance was not at first glance the easiest start to post-devolution life. However, several elements of the Conservatives' poor standing in Wales in 1997 and the lack of a sharply defined Welsh nationalism may have contributed to the circumstances that made party change possible. Compared with Scotland, the Welsh Conservatives may have had less money, machinery and independent history, but this also meant they went into devolution with less baggage.

The Welsh nation and administrative devolution

In Scotland in 1999, a Parliament was, in the words of Winifred Ewing at its opening, 'reconvened'. In Wales, the creation of the Assembly was always in part a political nation-building project. Campaigners for Welsh autonomy have throughout the history of administrative devolution (and even into the late life of the Assembly) used the example of Scotland to argue for similar arrangements in Wales (see, for example, Commission on Devolution in Wales, 2011). Parity with Scotland has been a constant theme of Welsh distinctiveness (see, for instance, Roberts, 2008; Mitchell, 2009: 48, 50, 66).

The Welsh Office and the post of Secretary of State for Wales were created in 1964. Although the Welsh Office was set up along the same lines as the Scottish Office, a senior civil servant confided to Morgan and Mungham (2000: 63–64) that it tended to be less self-confident than the Scottish Office and in the main went with the flow of Whitehall thinking. The Welsh Office habitually 'Welshified' policies and practices from across Whitehall for implementation in Wales, rather than pursuing the Welsh agenda in other parts of the machine (Rhodes, 1988: 149). In contrast to his own position as Secretary of State for Wales, Nicholas Edwards[1] notes 'the extraordinary effectiveness of the Scottish input into Cabinet decision-making' (Crickhowell, 1999: 60), particularly over the future of the Ravenscraig steel works and finance.[2]

The Welsh Office gradually built up functions over the course of its existence and became a key part of the model of administrative devolution through which the UK Government attempted to deal with territorial distinctiveness before 1999. For instance: powers of agriculture were given in 1979; a devolved budget system was established in 1980; and the Welsh councils for further and higher education were set up in 1993 (Richard Commission, 2004: 8). However, despite this growth, particularly under Nicholas Edwards and Sir Hywel Evans (Permanent Secretary, 1971–1980), it remained 'a minor office whose senior politicians and officials succeeded in avoiding controversy' (Mitchell, 2009: 62). Nevertheless, as Morgan (1999: 209) notes, 'the Welsh Office in the 18 years of Conservative rule, even if run by a sequence of Englishmen ... quietly changed the terms in which Welsh issues were considered. Almost by stealth, the Welsh Office's extended role after 1979 reinforced the sense of the territorial identity of Wales'.

The Conservative Party and the Welsh nation

Organisationally and politically, the Conservative Party did not in the main see Wales as a separate entity. There was some suggestion of a move towards a more distinctive attitude to Wales in the 1950s. *The Conservative Policy for Wales and Monmouthshire* published in March 1949 represented an opening for the Conservatives (Bale, 2012: 32). However, as so often with the Conservative Party and territorial statecraft, an opportunity to emerge ahead of the curve and shape events was missed. As Melding (2009: 179) recounts:

> It was in the 1950s that the Conservative Party came closest to reconstructing itself as an indigenous Welsh political party. Inspired by the *Policy for Wales* the Party's officers and several of its MPs believed that the Labour Party's hegemony could be broken by a popular Tory message that championed the cultural interests of Wales. Although London was not hostile to such a development, the UK Party failed to take the necessary measures to facilitate its outcome.

In particular, the failure to be the first to appoint a cabinet-level Secretary of State for Wales made the party look grudging in its acceptance of growing administrative devolution. The compromise of a proposal for a Minister of State for Welsh Affairs failed to recognise the inevitable move towards the deepening of administrative devolution. The Tories could have been seen to be the driving force behind this type of change, rather than the Government who accepted the inevitable after the event.

The appointment of secretaries of state for Wales representing English constituencies (and shadow secretaries of state during 1997–2010) also says something about the way Wales was treated at the centre of the Conservative Party. Such a situation would have been unthinkable in Scotland, even before 1979. For David Melding (2009: 93), the appointment of Peter Walker in 1987, was 'as if one of the later Holy Roman Emperors had forced the election of a Protestant as Pope'. Such a 'colonial practice', he argues, did lasting damage to the Welsh Conservatives and to unionist arguments.

Nevertheless, with the notable exception of John Redwood (1992–1995), most Conservative Welsh Secretaries adopted a sensitive and consensual approach. Nicholas Edwards recalls that, although she never quite understood Wales, Margaret Thatcher gave him a free hand at the Welsh Office (Crickhowell, 1999: 52), with which he pursued an industrial policy to his own taste (Crickhowell, 1999: 34–42). Similarly, Peter Walker accepted the office on the specific understanding that he would be able to pursue a distinctive approach, involving working with unions and industry in a much more proactive way than Thatcher would ever have contemplated (Bradbury, 1997: 88). He made it clear to Margaret Thatcher that he would be pursuing a more Heathite approach: 'I was allowed to do it my way with a range of interventionist policies and I always had her backing' (Walker, 1991: 203), including in the negotiation of a more generous public spending settlement for Wales in

Table 4.1 Conservative electoral performance in Wales at Westminster elections

Year	Votes	Percentage share	MPs
1966	396,795	27.9	3
1970	419,884	27.7	7
1974 (February)	412,535	25.9	8
1974 (October)	367,230	23.9	8
1979	526,254	32.2	11
1983	499,310	31	14
1987	501,316	29.5	8
1992	499,677	28.6	6
1997	317,145	19.6	0
2001	288,665	21	0
2005	297,830	21.4	3
2010	382,730	26.1	8
2015	407,813	27.2	11

Source: Rallings and Thrasher (2009); BBC News (2010a, 2015).

1988. However, although Walker undoubtedly pursued an agenda that suited better the political mood in Wales, it is less clear that he understood the idea of Wales as a nation, beyond supporting specific measures for the Welsh language. He knew 'what a lovely language Welsh was' (Walker, 1991: 204). He would also 'travel down to the Principality on the morning train from Paddington each week' (Walker, 1991: 205). Such a paternalistic attitude towards Wales was well meant but increasingly out of step with a growing sense of Welsh identity. Under David Hunt, another MP for an English constituency, this differentiation from English policy was continued. Overall, for Gamble (1993: 83), 'under Walker and Hunt the Welsh Office has practised not the disengagement favoured by Thatcherite ideology but an interventionist industrial policy'.

However, the appointment of John Redwood to the Welsh Office in 1992 signalled a likely departure from this approach. He was neither from the left of the Conservative Party, nor particularly noted for his accommodating approach. In reality, he was constrained by the inheritance of the policies set in train by his predecessors, but he did attempt to apply New Right ideas across all policy areas. He tried to promote small and medium sized enterprises and hived off more work from the Welsh Office to executive agencies. He also stopped proposals to strengthen the Welsh Grand Committee along the lines of its Scottish counterpart (Bradbury, 1997: 92). Overall, he was a Thatcherite minister who thought the best answer for Wales was a more assimilationist set of policies with England, but who did not understand Wales or Welsh sensitivities.

Hague's appointment to the Welsh Office in 1995 signalled another change of direction, but not wholly back to the approach adopted by Walker and Hunt. As Bradbury (1997: 93) notes, 'like Forsyth in Scotland, he balanced policy assimilationism with a more profoundly pro-Unionist rhetoric and respect for the union-state characteristics of Wales' governing arrangements'. He revisited several of John Redwood's most controversial policies: budget cuts for the Countryside Council for Wales were reversed; he commissioned an inquiry into child abuse in North Wales care homes; and strengthened the powers of the Welsh Grand Committee (Nadler, 2000: 160–161, 166–167). Nevertheless he remained implacably opposed to devolution, telling the House of Commons that an Assembly would be 'a waste of time, a waste of space and a waste of money. It would weaken not strengthen the position of Wales in the United Kingdom' (HC Hansard, 17 June 1996, col 507).

Increasingly, the manner in which the Conservatives governed Wales came to be seen as at best unsatisfactory and at worst illegitimate. First, the quango state in Wales came to be perceived as a way for Conservatives to bypass their electoral weakness to appoint sympathetic people to key positions. A series of scandals contributed to an impression that this type of arm's length governance had gone too far in Wales and this was a very contentious issue after 1997 and in the Assembly's first term (Morgan and Mungham, 2000: 45; Melding, 2009: 172).

Second, the artificial way in which Conservative policies were able to be implemented in Wales without a Welsh majority led to some of them losing touch with the prevailing policy mood. In Jonathan Evans' view, for instance, had Conservative policy been made in Wales, then it is unlikely both that the nursery voucher scheme would have been implemented and that the restructuring of Welsh local government would have taken the controversial course adopted (Evans, 2002: 24). One of the first symbolic (and cathartic) acts of Ron Davies as Secretary of State for Wales in 1997 was to immediately scrap the nursery voucher scheme (Morgan and Mungham, 2000: 67–68).

Overall, it is difficult to disagree with Melding's (2009: 178) conclusion that the Conservative Party's record in Wales 'can be summarised as one of failure flecked with intimations of promise'. In the main, Conservative commitment to Welsh distinctiveness was shown through legislation to protect the Welsh language. The idea of Wales as a nation did not enter into Conservative thinking. The Conservative Party lost all of its Welsh MPs in 1997 and did not gain any back until 2005.

The evolution of devolution in Wales, 1997–2011

Political institutions rarely emerge purely from considerations of what arrangements might be optimal. Instead, they reflect the result of bargaining and negotiating, particularly in political parties (Hopkin, 2003). In the case of Welsh devolution in 1997, this resulted in 'a compromise with few real friends' (Mitchell, 2009: 160–161). Above all else, it reflected the deep unease in the Labour Party about devolution, in particular due to the scars the party still bore from its 1970 experience (Wyn Jones and Scully, 2012: 42). The tortuous history of Welsh devolution affected the processes of change in the Conservative Party so it is briefly discussed here. As in Scotland, the Welsh Conservatives interpreted the outcome of the 1979 devolution referendum as a rejection of devolution once and for all (Melding, 2009: 105, 118; Torrance, 2009: 31–32).

It became clear from an early stage that the devolution arrangements proposed by the Labour Party in 1997 were unsatisfactory. As Wyn Jones and Scully (2012: 42) point out, there began almost immediately in 1997 a cross-party process of trying to improve the Assembly and its powers. The executive devolution model arose out of an internal Labour Party compromise after a debate about the need for primary legislative powers (Davies, 2002). Initially, a local government style chamber was changed to accommodate a cabinet model (National Assembly for Wales, 2002; Laffin and Thomas, 2003). Convinced that further change would be required to strengthen Welsh devolution, the Liberal Democrats insisted on the establishment of a commission to report on future options in their coalition agreement with the Labour Party in 2000. The Commission on the Powers and Electoral Arrangements for the National Assembly for Wales was established under the chairmanship of Lord Richard (a Labour peer) in July 2004.

Table 4.2 Welsh Assembly Governments since 1999

Dates	Type of Government
1999–2000	Labour minority
2000–2003	Labour and Liberal Democrat coalition
2003–2005	Labour majority
2005–2007	Labour minority
2007–2011	Labour and Plaid Cymru coalition
2011–	Labour majority

Lord Richard's report (2004) outlined a forensic and scathing critique of the way the Welsh Assembly was organised. At a public event to launch his report, Lord Richard summarised his view of the arrangements for Welsh devolution in 2004 as 'grotesque' (Wyn Jones and Scully, 2012: 43). His report recommended: that the Welsh Assembly should explicitly institute a parliamentary model of operation with a clear split between the executive and the rest of the chamber; that the Welsh Assembly should have primary law-making powers over the areas where it already had responsibility; and that the number of Assembly Members (AMs) should be increased to 80 and elected using the Single Transferable Vote System (STV; Richard Commission, 2004).

The report went further in its recommendations than many observers had predicted. However, as has always been the case with devolution in Wales, implementation depended on how internal arguments within the Labour Party played out. In the event, the Government of Wales Act 2006 ignored the recommendations about STV and increasing the number of AMs, but did pass primary law-making powers to the Assembly, subject to a confirmative vote in a future referendum to be held when two-thirds of the Assembly requested it and the UK Parliament and Secretary of State for Wales agreed (Part IV of the Act).

As Wyn Jones and Scully (2012: 49) have pointed out, the case for holding such a referendum, beyond placating anti-devolutionist opinion in the Labour Party, was not a strong one. In the interim, a series of Legislative Consent Orders (LCOs) would allow the Assembly to pass primary legislation on areas devolved to it by the UK Parliament on a case-by-case basis. Thus, in effect, the principle of the Assembly making primary law had already been conceded before the Welsh people had a chance to vote on it. However, the LCO system was widely regarded as cumbersome and ineffective (Miers, 2011: 9).

A condition of the coalition agreement between the Labour Party and Plaid Cymru in 2007 was that the Assembly should request that the UK Government initiate the process for having a referendum on Part IV of the Government of Wales Act, 2006, and that such a referendum should be held 'as soon as practicable, at or before the end of the Assembly term' (Osmond, 2007: 98). The referendum was duly held on 3 March 2011 with major figures in all political parties (including the Conservatives) campaigning for a positive result (63.5 per cent yes; 36.5 per cent no).

This long evolution was significant because it created a series of opportunities for the Conservative Party to engage constructively with Welsh devolution. Whilst the powers of the Scottish Parliament were widely accepted by the unionist parties (at least up to 2007) as meaningful and appropriate, from the outset the structure and remit of the Welsh Assembly were contested.

Drivers of party change for the Welsh Conservatives

Having outlined the context of post-devolution Welsh politics and the Conservative Party's inheritance, this chapter now turns to examine the potential drivers of change for the Welsh Conservatives described in Chapter 2. In the end, the greatest driver of party change for the Welsh Conservatives was a change of leadership. As for the Scottish Conservatives, devolution prompted practical organisation change. However, it also had a wider impact in forcing the Welsh Conservative Party to think seriously for the first time about being a separate entity.

Devolution as an external shock

Devolution acted as an external shock for the Welsh Conservatives both because they were forced to adapt organisationally and because they were forced to consider themselves for the first time as a more explicitly separate party. This was significant insofar as it caused those in the party who had campaigned against devolution to reassess the Conservative Governments (1979–1997) and their own idea about Wales as a nation (see, for instance: Evans, 2001; Bourne, 2005; Melding, 2009).

Change in dominant faction or leadership

Unlike in the Scottish Conservative Party, one leadership election in the Welsh Conservative Party can be said to have been decisive in driving party change. However, such change was not immediate and it was not announced with fanfare. Rather, the election of Nick Bourne as leader of the Welsh Conservatives set in train a series of changes that culminated in the party being on the cusp of entering coalition government with Plaid Cymru and the Liberal Democrats in 2007.

Pre-1997 factions in the Welsh Conservative Party

Factionalism in the Welsh Conservative Party tended, as in Scotland, to be played out on a UK level. As we have noted, most Conservative secretaries of state for

Wales generally steered clear of controversy and found a way to govern Wales which was, albeit on a certain set of terms, sensitive and consensual. The main factional arguments in the UK Conservative Party therefore played themselves out in Wales only insofar as it became under David Hunt and Peter Walker an example of how a non-Thatcherite alternative might be implemented. There did not before 1997 exist a faction in the Welsh Conservative Party arguing forcefully for a more Wales-centred approach that may have gone so far as to suggest that the party support devolution.

Beyond the constitutional arguments and the Conservatives' commitment to the Union, the model proposed for devolution in 1997 was deeply unsatisfactory and perhaps even counter-productive. Thus, even the most ardent pro-devolution Conservative might have found it extremely difficult to support such an arrangement, particularly considering the implications for finance and accountability. It was specifically William Hague's pitch to the Welsh electorate during the 1997 referendum campaign that what they were being offered should be rejected not only on its merits, but also because it was not the same form of devolution which was being offered to Scotland:

> Why do they want to give the Edinburgh Parliament the powers to legislate but not the Cardiff Assembly? Why do they trust Scots to decide whether they want tax-raising powers, but not the Welsh? A Welsh Assembly would represent the worst of both words. Wales would be deprived of its influence in the UK without gaining a direct say over its own affairs. (Hague, 1997)

Moreover, in contrast to Scotland where every single Scottish Labour MP with one exception (see Dalyell, 2012) signed the Claim of Right, the Welsh Labour Party was, and remains in some quarters, deeply ambivalent about devolution. The Welsh Conservatives did not find themselves on the wrong side of the 'settled will of the Welsh people'. Rather, in campaigning for a No vote, their position was much more mainstream than opposition to devolution could be portrayed in Scotland.

Transition from Richards to Bourne

Initially, in the absence of any Welsh MPs, William Hague appointed Jonathan Evans as the Conservative Party's chief spokesman on Wales. However, after he left to seek election to the European Parliament, Nick Bourne was appointed to the position. A subsequent election among party members was held for what was in effect the leadership of the emerging Welsh Conservative Party: the National Assembly Campaign Leader. In this election, Rod Richards beat the more 'establishment' candidate, Nick Bourne (Jones, 2001: 115–116). Richards was known to be more anti-devolution than Bourne and had a more combative political style.[3] For Melding (2012: 176), the absence of Jonathan Evans represented another missed opportunity for the party: 'It is unlikely that Jonathan Evans would have faced a serious challenge for the leadership and the Party would have adopted a centrist approach and set itself the challenge of locating the optimum centre-right position on the *Welsh* political spectrum.'

However, in September, Richards was accused of causing grievous bodily harm to a young woman (BBC News, 1999). Although he was subsequently cleared, at the time he resigned the leadership of the Welsh Conservative Party after Conservative AMs failed to back his choice of David Davies as deputy leader. Nick Bourne was appointed as an interim leader and then attained this position permanently when no other candidates were nominated to strand against him in a leadership election. At this time there were few hints about the direction in which he proposed to take the Welsh Conservatives, although it was clear that he took an altogether more accommodating view of devolution than Richards. This strategy may be contrasted with Murdo Fraser's leadership campaign in 2011 in which he laid all of his cards on the table. It is in this sense more similar to David Cameron's leadership campaign in 2005 that hinted at the direction of travel in extremely broad strokes (Denham and Dorey, 2005).[4]

For Tim Bale, at a UK level, 'a change of leadership in the Conservative Party is, in effect, regime change' (Bale, 2010: 17). The outcome of this episode was that a more moderate faction of the Welsh Conservative Party took control (including other AMs such as David Melding and Jonathan Morgan). However, even under the more pro-devolution leadership of Nick Bourne, change was slow and incremental. In 2000, the Conservative Assembly group remained deeply divided about devolution and at this stage the Scottish Conservatives had made more progress in moving on from opposition to devolution (Bradbury, 2006: 232–233). Even in 2004, Bourne was (publicly) sceptical about the Richard Commission's recommendations. He said that the Conservatives 'oppose any suggestion that the Assembly should be given law-making and tax-raising powers' and that any more powers for the Assembly would require a referendum (BBC News, 2004; Shipton, 2011: 133). It was not until much further down the path from the initial critical juncture of the transition to Bourne's leadership that its potential to drive change becomes evident. If Richards had remained as leader, it is unlikely that such a strategy would have been adopted.

Although we must bear in mind that *post hoc* explanations for party change may in part reflect a desire to construct a neat or positive narrative, it is certainly the case that Conservative elites view the replacement of Richards with Bourne as leader as a key turning point in the post-devolution history of the party. For one AM:

> David Cameron has done to the Conservative Party what Nick Bourne and his colleagues did to the Welsh Conservative Party here in Wales over the last ten years. Again, changed people's perceptions of the Welsh Conservative Party and again detoxified the brand. (Interview with Conservative AM 3, 1 March 2012)

Similarly, for another:

> Well, you have to give credit to Nick, he was the leader. And I think I could say personally he was probably in favour of it [a more 'Welsh' agenda], there was little doubt about that and was quite able then to facilitate discussion and agreement. I was a little bit sceptical myself, but when you see the facts, as it were, and let's say there was contention about where our votes would come from, when they were actually replicated in elections, both at local authority level, our parliamentary vote as well, I mean they are all part of it, just showed it was the right strategy for us to adopt and it worked in terms of our increasing numbers. (Interview with Conservative AM 2, 28 February 2012)

Thus, although the election of Nick Bourne was not the only driver of party change, and certainly was not alone in his view about the necessary future direction of the party, he did create the support at the top required to change the party's attitude to devolution and to how Welsh it should appear.

Electoral defeat

The resounding electoral defeat of the Conservative Party in 1997 prompted some in the party to fundamentally reconsider their positions. However, beyond moving slowly towards a slightly more accommodative approach under Nick Bourne and accepting the modest organisational changes to create a Welsh Conservative Party, this did not have much impact (Bradbury, 2006: 232).

In Clywd West, for instance, a seat which the Conservatives might have been expected to win back, the candidate selection before the 2001 general election may have damaged their chances. Instead of opting for their Welsh-speaking economics spokesman in the Assembly, local party members chose instead a retired army major from Northamptonshire who did not live in the constituency (Shipton, 2011: 70). The impression that the Conservatives may not fully have grasped the realities of devolution was compounded when they appointed Nigel Evans MP (Ribble Valley) to be the election coordinator in 2001 (Shipton, 2011: 72). William Hague had previously appointed a constitutional affairs spokesperson with a junior spokesperson for Wales rather than a Shadow Secretary of State for Wales. He then also appointed Nigel Evans as a Vice Chairman of the Party in charge of Wales, a move that Jonathan Evans was 'at a loss in trying to understand' (Evans, 2002: 26–27).

After the second general election in a row where the Conservative Party returned not a single Welsh MP to Westminster, Welsh AM David Melding tried to spark a debate on the necessary changes for recovery. In a speech to party members, he called for the party to move towards greater autonomy and perhaps copy the more devolved structure of the Scottish Conservative Party (Melding, 2001). However, although a review led by Wyn Roberts was commissioned and reported in 2002, it found no consensus on the need for change and party structures remained the same (Bradbury, 2006: 232; Roberts, 2008).

Electoral success, however, served to cement a narrative among party elites (and in newspapers and political commentary more generally, especially in Scottish Conservative circles) that the strategy pursued by Nick Bourne was the correct one. In particular, results from the 2007 Welsh Assembly election and the 2009 European Parliament elections were viewed as vindication for Bourne's leadership and his pursuit of a more 'Welsh' identity for the party. This in turn gave Bourne after 2007 even more license to make changes to the party's image and policies.

However, in discussing elections, it is important also to be mindful of the electoral context and party system in which parties operate. There was a sense in which this made change come more naturally to the Welsh Conservatives. First, the nationalist threat was not as strong in Wales as it was in Scotland (Melding, 2012: 130). According to one party official, this meant that nationalist voters were seen as less of a threat and more of an opportunity:

> Now, the difference I think in Wales is that you've got a much weaker nationalist voice than you do with the SNP. It's very much divided between the centre-right heritage voters and the socialist voters. And they are both quite vocal, which isn't the SNP. I mean obviously the SNP seems to show a much more united front. The other issue is that the softer nationalist vote in Plaid Cymru is amenable to voting Conservative on its regional vote, perhaps not in the constituency, so that has enabled us to gain

Table 4.3 Welsh Conservative performance at National Assembly elections

Constituency

Year	Votes	Percentage share	Number of AMs
1999	162,133	15.8	1
2003	169,832	19.9	1
2007	218,730	22.4	5
2011	237,389	25	6

Regional list

Year	Votes	Percentage share	Number of AMs
1999	168,206	16.5	8
2003	162,725	19.2	10
2007	209,153	21.4	7
2011	213,773	22.6	8

Source: Rallings and Thrasher (2009); National Assembly for Wales (2011).

more seats than perhaps we might have done. (Interview with Welsh party official 1, 26 March 2013)

Second, supporting an improved or more powerful Welsh Assembly involved fewer compromises with an established view of unionism than it did in Scotland. It was not as controversial to be on board with changes to an institution that was widely seen as unsatisfactory. As one Conservative AM explains:

> Now, I think what the key thing here is that it created a gap really for the Welsh Conservative Party ... to suddenly get on board with part of the devolution project because it was so incomplete that it still had to be won, and this in the end led to a position where nearly all the group campaigned for a Yes vote in 2011. The party, despite the reservations of some senior members in the voluntary party and perhaps at a UK level, certainly amongst our membership, accepted that we had neutrality, which I think was a big shift from where we were culturally before. But neutrality in effect meant that all the prominent Welsh Conservatives who were in the campaign were on the yes side, so these were big, big opportunities for us to get on board the devolution project, which forever history will record that this pretty robust choice was presented for Scotland in 1997, the Scottish Conservative Party said no, and we said no to a much weaker model and then said yes to strengthening it and having a proper balanced robust institution so again I think amongst elites, certainly the journalists, how far this penetrates to your average voter is another issue, but I think it has been a big factor in the success we have had at rebranding. (Interview with Conservative AM 6, 2 March 2012)

Overall, electoral defeat was less important than changes in leadership and dominant faction for party change in the Welsh Conservatives. However, crucially, the new dominant faction found the circumstances easier than those in Scotland.

Political opportunity structure

Unlike in Scotland, there was a very clear path for the Conservatives to be in government in Wales. The smaller Welsh Assembly and the Welsh party system meant that any coalition arrangement that did not involve the Labour Party had to involve the Conservatives. Thus, if the other parties wanted the Labour Party to be out of office, they had no choice but to consider how they could work with the Welsh Conservatives.

This placed a responsibility not only on the other parties, but also on the Welsh Conservative Party itself. If it wanted to see a change of Government in Wales, then it had to be prepared to be a part of it. Thus, if there were no change of Government in Wales, then it would in part be the fault of the Conservative Party for failing to form one. In order to do so, it would have to make itself a viable coalition partner for two parties of the centre-left. This was clearly a difficult proposition for the Welsh Conservatives. However, crucially, it was one that held out the realistic possibility of office. Unlike in Scotland, the other parties could not afford to ignore the Conservative Party if they wanted to form a Government without Labour. They, too, therefore had an incentive to reconsider their previous hostility towards the Conservatives. The political opportunity structure for both the Conservatives and other parties was completely different in Scotland.

Manifestations of party change

Having entered the Welsh Assembly with a stance which was arguably even more reluctant than the Scottish Conservatives in 1999, the Welsh Conservatives began a much more far-reaching process of party change under the leadership of Nick Bourne. Initial fears in 1999 that the Conservatives were 'in danger of becoming the most destructive force in the Assembly' (Morgan and Mungham, 2000: 212) were forgotten when the Conservatives managed to move themselves into a position where they were on the cusp of being in government in Wales. This section explains how they managed to do so. Although the extent of party change in Wales can be exaggerated the evidence points to significant differences between the Welsh Conservatives in 1999 and in 2011. These are most acute in policy and presentation, but considerably less so in terms of party organisation. This section therefore also seeks to explore how a party with less formal autonomy and virtually no separate history managed to more wholeheartedly embrace a more 'nationalist' and pro-devolution agenda.

Party organisation

The Welsh Conservatives were formed through territorial penetration, rather than territorial consolidation (Eliassen and Svaasand, 1975: 16; Panebianco, 1988: 51). It is much more difficult to talk of an indigenous Welsh Conservatism (Bradbury, 2006). While Seldon and Ball's (1994) overview of the *Conservative Century* devotes one chapter to Scotland, Wales does not merit separate consideration. Similarly, in John Major's (1999) autobiography, Wales is hardly mentioned, but Scotland and the Union receives a full chapter of consideration. It was only after devolution that a somewhat separate Welsh party began to emerge. However, the extent of separation from the English Conservative Party was, on paper, very limited. Instead, the Welsh Conservatives have exploited the de facto policy autonomy they were given in order to pursue a different path.

The creation of a Welsh Conservative Party?

Although the Conservative Party produced separate manifestos for Wales at Westminster elections, the party remained very much integrated with the English Conservative Party. For Melding, 'the Conservative Party in Wales became an utterly derivative entity without even the modest autonomy usually given to a branch franchise' (Melding, 2009: 170). After the successful devolution referendum in 1997, the Conservative Party reorganised itself in Wales and Scotland. However, Wales did not receive anything like the same autonomy as Scotland. It is created by one line in the constitution of the UK Conservative Party: 'There shall be established and maintained in Wales The Welsh Conservative Party which shall be managed by a Board (known as "the Board for Wales")' (Conservative Party, 2009: 69).

Beyond the creation of this board, it is difficult to say that a separate Welsh organisation exists. However, even this board is viewed as limited in scope. Jonathan Evans suggested in 2002 that it should be 'fully under the control and remit of the Welsh Conservative Party' (Evans, 2002: 29). When asked whether the Welsh board was the equivalent of a Welsh central office one AM was happy to say that 'decisions are made in Wales' (interview with Conservative AM 3, 1 March 2012). Others were much more circumspect:

> Yes, it is. It is and it isn't. It's the voluntary party and it is made up of representatives from each of the areas. The councillors, I forget all the others now, but that's how it is drawn together. And one of our problems, if you research it, is you will see the same people have had office for the last 12 years in varying positions. That, to my mind, is very unhealthy, in any organisation. (Interview with Conservative AM 1, 27 February 2012)

Similarly, for another AM:

> I think that board has been disappointing because it's not been able to really make a theoretical measure of autonomy work functionally and really the board takes its directions pretty much from London. The secretariat, they are line managed in effect from London, there isn't enough independence in our structure and that gets tested at certain times. It's not usually a problem in the day-to-day workings of a party, it's a fairly bureaucratic organisation. (Interview with Conservative AM 6, 2 March 2012)

Table 4.4 Structure of the Welsh Conservative Party

Board of the Welsh Conservative Party
Party Chairman
Political Deputy Chairman   Membership Deputy Chairman
Area Chairmen
Conservative Leader in the Welsh Assembly
Chairman of Welsh Local Government Committee
Director for Wales (non-voting)
(Shadow) Secretary of State for Wales
Member of the European Parliament

Source: Conservative Party (2009: 69–70).

One indication of the lack of a separate party structure in Wales occurred in 2012 when the Welsh Party board abruptly decided to cancel the Welsh Conservative Party conference with two weeks' notice. The party said it was for reasons of cost and the conference was instead replaced with a one-day 'rally' (BBC News, 2012b).

Moreover, despite having had a leadership election that was widely referred to as the contest for the 'leadership of the Welsh Conservative Party', technically David Cameron is the leader of the Welsh Conservative Party. When the author put it to a Conservative AM that this was a 'Cardiff Bay bubble' issue with little relevance to voters or day-to-day politics, he pointed to the wider symbolism of the anomaly: 'I put this to you: if there was genuine organisational independence or autonomy, a federal body, let's put it that way for ease, would the party have cancelled its annual conference in Wales? I mean what political parties cancel their own conferences?' (interview with Conservative AM 6, 2 March 2012). This situation is more widely perceived as unsatisfactory:

> It makes sense to me that if we have got a Scottish leader in Scotland. I understand that we will have a Northern Ireland leader, then it makes sense that we should have a Welsh leader as well. And I think probably over the last ten years people, have up until last year, Nick was our group leader and I think most people in Wales saw him as the Welsh Conservative leader, but of course he wasn't leader of the Welsh Conservatives, but I want to see that happening. I think that will happen because I think that is inevitable. So in my opinion I think Andrew who has actually been elected by the members of the Welsh Conservative Party should in my opinion be leader of the Welsh Conservative Party because that makes sense. (Interview with Conservative AM 3, 1 March 2012)

Similarly but less emphatically:

> There is the leadership of the party, the leader of the party in Wales at the moment is currently David Cameron and I am very happy with that, but if there was a discussion at some point in the future about changing that, then that would be a good discussion to have. (Interview with Conservative AM 2, 29 February 2012)

Andrew R.T. Davies, the leader of the Welsh Conservative group in the Assembly, has also called for this change (Wales Online, 2012). It is still therefore difficult to say that an entirely separate Welsh organisation exists. However, as we observed with the Scottish Conservatives, it is essential in the study of political parties to delve deeper than the formal organisation and into the *enacted* organisation. In practice, the Welsh Conservatives have had almost complete policy autonomy and have used this to project a distinct image despite their lack of a separate party organisation.

Territorial organisational autonomy

Although the Welsh Conservatives may on paper appear to have less autonomy than the Scottish Conservatives, in reality they have been given the same level of freedom as their Scottish colleagues in most areas.

Leadership selection

In contrast with the Welsh Labour Party (see Hopkin, 2009: 186–187), there have been no instances where the central UK Conservative Party has attempted to interfere with Welsh Conservative leadership selection. Rod Richards won the first election in 1998; Nick Bourne was elected unopposed; and Andrew R.T. Davies won the 2011 contest. There is no evidence that the central party acted to endorse a preferred candidate.

Candidate selection

In 1999, the Welsh Conservatives devised their own procedures for selecting candidates for the new Welsh Assembly and for ranking them in order for the party list element of the electoral system (Bradbury *et al.*, 2000: 67–68). There were some differences between Wales and Scotland in this regard. However, as Bradbury *et al.* (2000: 69) note: 'those differences arose from the accumulated autonomy of the Scottish and Welsh offices of the party, rather than from any dynamic process of decentralisation to accompany devolution'. Almost by default, therefore, initial candidate selection was carried out in Wales. Unlike in the Labour Party, there were no arguments about gender balance or central interference. Procedures in 2003 were much the same, with only one de-selection carried out by the Welsh party (Mitchell and Bradbury, 2004).

However, the Welsh Conservative Party is not fully in charge of candidate selection for Westminster seats. Like in England and Northern Ireland (but in contrast to Scotland), Welsh constituency associations must select from the UK approved list of candidates (Conservative Party, 2009: 29).

Policy-making autonomy

Before 1997, if the Welsh Conservative Party lacked a separate organisational identity before devolution, then its lack of policy differentiation was even more marked. Policies were in general made at a UK level and then translated to Wales. There existed the legal and political entity of 'England and Wales'.

However, there is evidence that the Welsh Office had leeway when it came to policies which affected Wales only or which had of necessity to be given a specific Welsh character. For instance, during the negotiations about the new national curriculum in 1988, Wyn Roberts led the process for the Welsh Office and was able to ensure that the Welsh language was given a statutory place in schools for the first time (Roberts, 2006: 221–222). In the main policy differentiation was shown through commitment to the Welsh language (Melding, 2009: 125).

However, in the post-devolution period, this is the area where the Welsh Conservatives have the most freedom. In general, the UK Conservative Party has allowed them a free hand with policy-making for domestic Welsh issues. Whilst noting disagreements, one AM concludes that the Welsh party has almost complete independence in this area:

> I don't believe that they have a veto over policies we want to develop here. Yes, there are sometimes difficulties and disagreements and of course you'd expect that but that's devolution and I think we need to be relaxed about that. As I say to my colleagues: we need to chill. Because at the end of the day, yes, we will do things differently here in Wales because things will be done differently in England. We've got to recognise that and we've got to accept that and be relaxed about that and I think our colleagues at a London level realise that as well. (Interview with Conservative AM 3, 1 March 2013)

However, it is clear that some aspects of the Welsh Conservative Party's programme are subject to negotiation with the UK party:

> As you can imagine, the group here put together the policies for the National Assembly in terms of those matters which are devolved and then it is negotiated, shall we say ... Things that they didn't like, we had to vigorously defend and it was a reasonable compromise in the end. I suppose I would say that I wasn't aware of any major disagreements. There was a recognition that the evidence we put forward for those things that differed perhaps from national policy were well intentioned and were practical and capable of implementation. (Interview with Conservative AM 1, 27 February 2012)

Similarly, when asked explicitly if the Welsh party always prevailed in a disagreement with the UK party, another Conservative AM agreed, but added:

> I think that there is genuine policy autonomy, but that was expressed within still a very coherent UK Conservative Party and frequent discussions between the Shadow Secretary of State, now the Secretary of State, leader of the opposition, now the Prime Minister, Conservative Research Department, and whatever they are called now. All these things happen. So it would be wrong to project the policy personality we now have as somehow completely distinct from the party at a UK level, but the big decisions have gone our way and I think that's been good for us and good for the party on a UK basis as well. But some of those decisions have had to be quite hardly fought internally. (Interview Conservative AM 6, 2 March 2012)

For instance, on the issue of whether a future Conservative Government should support a referendum to unlock Part IV of the Government of Wales Act 2006, the UK party was initially reluctant to make any commitments. Indeed, it might even have been tempted to say that it would not hold a referendum in the lifetime of the first Parliament of a Conservative Government. However, when the Welsh party pointed out that a referendum would be triggered by a two-thirds majority in the Welsh Assembly and that it might not be politically wise to oppose such a request, the UK party speedily changed its mind (interview with Conservative AM 6, 2 March 2012).

No AM noticed any particular difference under successive Conservative leaders since 1997. There was a curious incident when it appeared that Michael Howard might attempt to impose Foundation Hospitals on Wales, but nothing subsequently came of this, apart from embarrassment and a sense that the UK party under his leadership had not yet fully come to terms with the reality of Welsh devolution (Shipton, 2011: 158–159). In 2013, one party official commented that relations with the UK party were much better: 'There is a real relaxation whenever we speak to colleagues in Downing Street or other government departments that, you know, we are the ones who are at the coal face, so we are the ones who make the decisions' (interview with Welsh official, 26 March 2013).

The party's Director of Policy, David Melding, controlled policy-making until he left this post in 2011. As Elias (2013: 21) notes, the policy-making process for the Welsh Conservatives mirrors the UK level in that is highly centralised and tightly controlled by party elites:

> This involves formulating policy documents in the key areas of Assembly competence, and putting these out to extensive consultation among party members as well as external civil society groups. Two policy conferences a year provide further opportunities to discuss these ideas, although few final policy decisions are taken here. Final manifesto approval is provided by a Welsh Management Board composed of representatives of the party's voluntary, elected and professional wings. Just as with Welsh Labour, the Welsh Conservatives' Annual Conference has no formal role in approving party policy.

This centralisation of policy-making capacity around the AM group is also a result of the fact that the Welsh Conservatives' Central Office does not have any policy research staff. As one party official observes:

> Policy development happens in this [Welsh Assembly] building because there is a greater competency now in the Assembly with the primary law making powers and possibly even fiscal power. So the structure has adapted, but not on the surface if that makes sense. (Interview with Welsh party official 1, 26 March 2013)

Thus, the formal organisational structures of the Welsh Conservative Party do not reflect the enacted organisation when it comes to making policy.

Finance

The Welsh Conservative Party is not financially self-sufficient and relies on funding from the UK party. This acts as a brake on ideas to separate the party from the UK Conservative Party. Although its finances are not constituted separately, one AM was very clear that further separation was not an option until the financial issue was resolved:

> There is no way in which we could ever come anywhere near the funding that comes to us from Westminster. Our membership is too small and we have no, to take the Scottish example, no major donor, never have had, not saying we won't do in the future. I mean, I'm not aware of anybody who would have the same influence as Lord Laidlaw as he is now, in that way. So though the aspiration is there, the other side of it, not just the finance side of it: the leadership side of it. (Interview with Conservative AM 1, 27 February 2012)

However, although he did not disagree about the nature of the funding situation, one Conservative AM argued for a bolder approach:

Well, if the Liberals can run a Welsh Liberal party. I mean, why be afraid of a little bit of genteel political poverty? You know, you'd have to adapt your structures a bit, but, you know, we'd still have the same members, we'd still have the same elections to fight. We might have to have a slightly more modest office, I don't know. But, good God, we're a party that doesn't believe in dependency cultures and here we are with the mother of all political dependency cultures. (Interview with Conservative AM 6, 2 March 2012)

Thus, financial considerations act as a brake on party change. However, it should be noted that other parties in Wales face similar financial predicaments.

Personnel

The weakness of the Welsh Party Board means that leadership in the Assembly became more important for the Welsh Conservatives. The main strategic and policy decisions are taken at the Assembly in Cardiff Bay, rather than in Welsh Conservative Central Office. There have been no major changes in personnel which have particularly caused party change over the period 1999–2011. However, it must be noted that the initial election in 1999 of AMs with an agenda for change is crucial in explaining party change for the Welsh Conservatives. Had AMs like David Melding and Nick Bourne not won election in 1999, then the history of the Welsh Conservatives might have been different. The weakness of the Welsh Conservative Party's extra-parliamentary structures means that the composition of the AM group is central to the direction of the party.

Table 4.5 Conservative Members of the Welsh Assembly, 1999–2011

Constituency	1999	2003	2007	2011
Monmouth	David Davies	David Davies	Nick Ramsey	Nick Ramsey
Cardiff North			Jonathan Morgan	
Carmarthen West and South Pembrokeshire			Angela Burns	Angela Burns
Clywd West			Darren Millar	Darren Millar
Preseli Pembrokeshire			Paul Davies	Paul Davies
Aberconwy				Janet Finch-Saunders
Montgomeryshire				Russell George

Table 4.5 (*cont.*)

Region

	1999	2003	2007	2011
Mid and West Wales	Nick Bourne Glyn Davies	Nick Bourne Glyn Davies	Nick Bourne	
North Wales	Rod Richards* Peter Rogers	Mark Isherwood Brynie Williams	Mark Isherwood Brynie Williams	Mark Isherwood Antoinette Sandbach
South Wales Central	David Melding Jonathan Morgan	David Melding Jonathan Morgan	David Melding Andrew R.T. Davies	David Melding Andrew R.T. Davies
South Wales East	William Graham	William Graham Laura Anne Jones	William Graham Mohammed Asghar	William Graham Mohammed Asghar
South Wales West	Alun Cairns	Alun Cairns	Alun Cairns	Bryon Davies Suzy Davies

* Rod Richards became an Independent Conservative in 2000 and resigned from the Assembly in 2002. He was replaced from 2002–2003 by David Jones.

Source: National Assembly for Wales (2013).

The ban on dual candidacy has resulted in unexpected changes in personnel. For instance, in 2011, Nick Bourne lost his seat because the party did so well at a constituency level in the Mid- and West Wales region. However, there have been no major changes in personnel akin to the new intake of Conservative MPs in 2010.

Policy

The most profound sense in which the Welsh Conservative Party has changed is in its policy platform and in its process of what one AM calls 'Welshification' (interview with Conservative AM 3, 1 March 2012). The extent to which it was willing to compromise in the coalition negotiations of 2007 demonstrated that the party had moved on significantly from its opposition to devolution in 1997. The Welsh Conservative Party moved from Rod Richards' leadership into a position where it was not considered impossible for it to be in coalition with Plaid Cymru.

This section analyses post-devolution Welsh policy through analysis of manifestos and statements. Finally, the idea of 'Welshification' is examined in detail, revealing it to be a conscious strategy (Melding, 2012: 130), but also one that was incremental and subject to the ebb and flow of everyday political concerns. Overall, party change in terms of policy in the Welsh Conservative Party is less qualified by the roots of British Conservatism (Hayton, 2012) than the UK or Scottish Conservative parties.

1999 manifesto

The 1999 Welsh Conservative Party manifesto is a brief document. It gives the overall impression of a manifesto written in a hurry without much thought or enthusiasm. Rod Richards makes the rather original point in his foreword that:

> Neither must devolution become a process that facilitates the creation of political union with Europe. The transfer of power from Westminster to Brussels would destroy our British identity and our British values. The transfer of further powers from Westminster to the Assembly would lead to the fragmentation of Britain, making European federalism easier for the government to achieve. (Welsh Conservative Party, 1999)

Policies are then outlined under the theme of 'fair play'. For instance, fair play in business means the rather under specified priority of: 'We will actively support small firms in all regions of Wales' (Welsh Conservative Party, 1999). In education, parental choice is central and it is also suggested that private companies should be allowed to take over failing schools, provided education remains free. In health: 'We believe in local community hospitals. They are what the people want – care close to home' (Welsh Conservative Party, 1999).

The 1999 manifesto is not a serious attempt to engage with the new institutions and it certainly does not buy into the spirit of a better Wales being created by the Assembly (such optimism is to be discouraged: 'Promises of a Welsh Utopia are as cruel as they are unfair'). Instead, it is a vague statement of Conservative principles which at best adopts a 'wait and see' approach to how the powers of the Assembly will unfold. The contrast with the moderate and open tone of the 1999 Scottish Conservative manifesto is stark.

2003 manifesto

The 2003 manifesto is, first, a more professional exercise. However, second, it also contains flashes of a much more distinctive approach for the party. Nick Bourne's foreword emphasises the key themes: 'the need to invest in our public services, to provide help to create Welsh jobs, to support rural Wales, to halt wasteful projects like the new Assembly building proposal, and invest the savings in public services' (Welsh Conservative Party, 2003: 1). This is a radically different agenda from that proposed in 1999. The 2003 manifesto is a detailed document with clear spending commitments and policies.

In health, patients are to be allowed to seek treatment privately if they are forced to wait too long, but the manifesto also emphasises strongly the need to invest in new staff and treatment centres. Targets will be toughened and Foundation Hospitals will be created in Wales. There is also perhaps a harbinger of Andrew Lansley's attempt to depoliticise the NHS in the Health and Social Care Act in the proposal to set up NHS Cymru as an independent delivery organisation for which the Assembly should set broad strategic objectives (Welsh Conservative Party, 2003: 5–6).

In education, there is an overarching theme of promoting choice and diversity through school specialisms and through a vague promise that parents should decide where to send their children. However, this is matched with detailed commitments in other areas. School budgets are to be ring-fenced and based on a three-year cycle (Welsh Conservative Party, 2003: 15). National testing is to be retained, but there will be a review of how to provide contextualised performance data (Welsh Conservative Party, 2003: 18). In particular, in higher education, the manifesto commits the Welsh Conservatives to asking the UK Government to devolve power over university tuition fees to Wales so that it can abolish tuition fees for Welsh students (Welsh Conservative Party, 2003: 20).

Social, children's and elderly care is given eight pages of attention, with detailed policies on helping carers and improving the system for looked-after children (Welsh Conservative Party, 2003: 24–31). In particular, the party commits itself to publishing a strategy to tackle child poverty (Welsh Conservative Party, 2003: 26) and a pilot of a 'unified care trust' to break down the barriers between health and social care (Welsh Conservative Party, 2003: 28).

The party now 'celebrates the fact that in today's Wales other sources of discrimination are now more readily acknowledged, including those based on age, religious beliefs and sexual orientation' (Welsh Conservative Party, 2003: 34). In this vein, it commits itself to ensuring that the UK Government recognises the importance of all the equality strands before proceeding to reform the UK's equality commissions (Welsh Conservative Party, 2003: 34).

In the section entitled 'An Enterprising Wales', the party outlines a moderate economic strategy: 'taxes limited; road and rail infrastructure improved; an excellent skills base; and a first-class telecommunications network' (Welsh Conservative Party, 2003: 38). This includes specific policies on Cardiff Airport and on the installation of broadband and goes beyond an agenda of tax cuts and deregulation. There are also to be tax credits for research and development investment in Wales (Welsh Conservative Party, 2003: 42).

On the constitution, the Welsh Conservatives outline an imaginative (if slightly convoluted) compromise. Instead of simply having an Assembly with law-making powers, the party proposes that a concordat be established with the Secretary of State for Wales which would: contain an agreement that matters substantially affecting Wales should only be put forward as Wales-only bills; that the relevant subject committee of the Assembly meets in joint session with the Welsh Grand Committee to discuss the second reading of Wales-only bills; and that Westminster should pass small matters of primary law which the Assembly requests in a General Provisions Bill (Welsh Conservative Party, 2003: 77). Such proposals are in some ways reminiscent of John Major's attempts to strengthen the Union under Ian Lang as Secretary of State for Scotland: they go as far as possible within existing arrangements without major constitutional change.

Throughout the document, the Conservatives explore ways to try to increase Wales' influence in the UK. For instance: ensuring that Wales is represented on the new contents board of Ofcom (p.70); establishing a national public records office for Wales (p.69); and providing strong Welsh input into decisions about tagging of sheep (p.48).

In particular, 2003 was an election in which the Conservatives appeared to benefit from playing to those in Wales who saw themselves as primarily British (Wyn Jones and Scully, 2004). Thus it would be wrong at this point to portray the Welshification of the Conservative Party as fully underway. As we have noted, Bourne gave an initially cool reception to the report of the Richard Commission and the manifesto specifically says that the Welsh Conservatives will not support more law-making powers: 'Parliament should remain the single law-making authority for Wales' (Welsh Conservative Party, 2003: 77, 79).

The 2007 manifesto: towards coalition

The 2007 Welsh Conservative manifesto marks an even more explicit claim to the centre ground of Welsh politics. However, some pre-1997 commitments remain and the document still reflects divides on the constitutional question. Indeed, the manifesto struck so moderate a tone that David Fouweather, a Conservative councillor in Newport, complained publicly that: 'I can't get a good number of people out working on the campaign. This is a wet, liberal manifesto that they don't want to sell on the doorstep' (Wales Online, 2007).

The manifesto begins by talking about the NHS: 'We are committed to improving the NHS for everyone, rather than helping the few to opt out' (Welsh Conservative Party, 2007: 7). The party commits itself to new spending on a cancer drugs fund and on a palliative care strategy. Highlighted sections draw attention to commitments on 'local GP services available when you need them' and 'an Order in Council from Westminster to allow the Assembly to pass a Mental Health Reform Measure' (Welsh Conservative Party, 2007: 7). On organisational issues, the Welsh Conservatives suggest a cross-party commission to chart a way forward for the Welsh NHS. However, they retain a commitment to GP practices playing a 'direct role in the commissioning of secondary services' (Welsh Conservative Party, 2007: 8).

On the economy, the manifesto aims to make Wales the 'most business friendly location in Europe'. Alongside an expanded business rate relief scheme financed through an investment fund, small and medium sized businesses would be rewarded for: meeting energy conservation targets; reducing use of motor vehicles; allowing flexible working, e.g. for people with caring responsibilities; and providing childcare (Welsh Conservative Party, 2007: 11). This section also concentrates on cohesion funding for West Wales and the Valleys, social enterprise and 'The Welsh Coastline – A Maritime Marvel' (Welsh Conservative Party, 2007: 12–13).

The section on a 'sustainable way of life' includes strong environmental commitments (Welsh Conservative Party, 2007: 15–17). On education ('Learning: The

Key to Success'), schools should receive their core funding directly from Cardiff, rather than from local education authorities on a three-year budgetary cycle (Welsh Conservative Party, 2007: 19). Apart from stating that 'a Welsh Conservative government would introduce a range of policies to encourage versatility, choice, and higher standards', the manifesto does not mention parental choice or different types of school (Welsh Conservative Party, 2007: 19). Instead it talks about closing the gap between per pupil spending in England and Wales and maintaining the requirement for schools to have school councils (Welsh Conservative Party, 2007: 20–21). Social justice again features heavily in commitments to 'housing for all' and 'an end to poverty' (Welsh Conservative Party, 2007: 24–25).

However, again the question of the future of the Assembly and devolution is fudged. The manifesto criticises the Labour Party's record, but suggests only a cross-party commission to look at the future of the devolved settlement.

The Rainbow Coalition and the All-Wales Accord

The 2007 Welsh Assembly elections were disastrous for the Labour Party. It suffered its worst result in Wales since 1918. Its safest seats were under threat from both Plaid Cymru and the Conservative Party. They fell one seat short of being able to govern again as a minority administration. The Conservatives won the constituency seats of Preseli Pembrokeshire, Carmarthen West and South Pembrokeshire, Clywd West and Cardiff North. However, it took two months before a coalition government was formed.

In particular, the Labour Party's attitude towards Plaid Cymru was critical in Plaid's decision to suspend coalition talks with them in order to pursue a 'Rainbow Coalition' with the Conservatives and Liberal Democrats. This was a quite unexpected configuration. John Osmond observes of the Conservatives that:

> they determined, in a way perhaps typical of a party that naturally aspires to government, that they must change or die. And change they did, almost effortlessly it seemed, embracing a Welsh patriotic agenda that went far beyond their well-established positive attitude to the language and culture to connect with a recognition of the Welsh political nation and the new relationships it would have to forge within the United Kingdom Union (rather than Unitary) State. (Osmond, 2007: 11)

After detailed negotiations, the three parties produced the *One-Wales Accord*. Much like the coalition negotiations after the 2010 general election, the three parties in fact found that there was much common ground and, crucially, that the Conservatives were willing to compromise significantly. For instance, both the Plaid Cymru and Liberal Democrat negotiators were surprised at how relaxed the Conservatives were about the nation-building aspects of the agreement (Osmond, 2007: 23).

On a referendum on transferring Part IV of the Government of Wales Act 2006, for example, the Conservatives were also able to compromise. As David Melding recalls:

> We could not officially endorse this in the sense that we could direct the membership to campaign in favour. However, we undertook that Cabinet Ministers would abide by collective responsibility and would, of course, campaign in favour. (Quoted in Osmond, 2007: 24)

On justice, although the Conservatives were unable to acquiesce to the full devolution of police and criminal justice, they offered instead youth justice (Osmond, 2007: 25). The other parties were also surprised about the extent to which policies on social justice converged. However, although the Conservatives received endorsement from their AM group, the Welsh Party Board and from the UK shadow cabinet to proceed, in the end the Liberal Democrats' Welsh Executive Committee was tied on the Rainbow Coalition and thus unable, despite a later vote in favour by the party's membership, to proceed. Plaid, who had also agreed the deal through their internal processes, then left to restart negotiations with the Labour Party.

One Conservative AM was quite clear that the Rainbow Coalition would have been workable:

> We could have done it, there is little doubt of that. There would have been difficulties with some of the aspects of Plaid. The Lib Dems, I think, you know what I mean, would eventually have come in to the thing, embraced it shall we say. The realities of government are very coalescing. It isn't just, how do I put it, the use of the ministerial limousine. It's far more with the effective use of power and that is all the Conservative Party is about. (Interview with Conservative AM 1, 27 February 2012)

Osmond (2007: 45) perhaps overstates his case about the change the coalition negotiations have wrought to say that: 'With the Welsh Conservatives Plaid Cymru now has a serious challenger in terms of identity politics.' Nevertheless, from the Conservatives' electoral nadir in 1997 and the 1999 manifesto, it is clear that the party had changed significantly in terms of its policies and tone. Melding (2012: 130) also reports that confidence-building measures between the Conservatives and the main opposition parties had taken place throughout the 2003–2007 Assembly term. There was thus a clear strategy to manoeuvre the Conservatives into a position where they could be considered a viable coalition partner.

2011 and future policy-making

The 2011 manifesto is a restatement of the type of policies and tone that the Conservatives adopted in 2007. Its main points are summarised at the beginning under the title *A New Voice for Wales*:

- Protect the NHS budget for the next 4 years.
- Invest in education to give teachers, parents and governors a greater say.
- Introduce an Armed Forces' Card to give benefits such as free bus travel and NHS priority care.
- Eliminate child poverty by 2020.
- Scrap business rates for all small businesses.
- Protect free bus passes and free prescriptions for older people.
- Protect flood plains with new 'Blue Belts' to prevent irresponsible development.
- Promote the Welsh language with a new Charter Mark for businesses that encourage its use (Welsh Conservative Party, 2011: 4).

Again, on the economy, beyond tax cuts the party also proposes 'a Welsh hub in London'; looking into the possibility of devolving Network Rail; at least four enterprise zones; and the establishment of a micro-credit scheme in disadvantaged areas (Welsh Conservative Party, 2011: 6–7).

In health, the party commits itself (following the UK party) to protect health spending and introduce a cancer drugs fund (Welsh Conservative Party, 2011: 8). In particular, ambulance services and stroke services are to be better funded. The party also proposes to appoint a Deputy Minister for Public Health (Welsh Conservative Party, 2011: 9). The internal market and the possibilities for greater private sector involvement are not mentioned.

In education, the manifesto slightly downplays its radicalism: the one line devoted to 'Fund schools directly from WAG [Welsh Assembly Government] to give headteachers the power to boost attainment' leaves open a lot of questions about removing Local Education Authorities completely from this process (Welsh Conservative Party, 2011: 11). Alongside this, the Welsh Conservatives would introduce a Welsh version of Teach First, retain the England and Wales pay structure for teachers, and introduce a 'pupil premium' to target money at schools with large numbers of disadvantaged children (Welsh Conservative Party, 2011: 11–12). Elsewhere, the manifesto lambasts what it terms Labour's failure on child poverty and commits the party to eliminate child poverty by 2020 and publish a strategy on how to improve the attainment of looked-after children (Welsh Conservative Party, 2011: 13–14).

In a special section on climate change, the party commits itself to a 3 per cent reduction in Welsh-sourced greenhouse gas emissions for devolved areas and to the promotion of renewable energy (Welsh Conservative Party, 2011: 15–16). In addition, a whole section is devoted to the theme of 'social justice', including proposals to support carers and reduce fuel poverty. In a section which very much echoes the Big Society themes of the UK party (see Conservative Party, 2010), the Welsh Conservatives propose to reduce ring-fenced grants to local authorities and hold referendums on directly-elected mayors for certain towns. The manifesto proposes to support the Welsh language by creating a Charter Mark for businesses that promote Welsh language services (Welsh Conservative Party, 2011: 26).

However, the 2011 manifesto also hints at the limits of party change for the Welsh Conservatives, particularly on the constitution. Although the manifesto proposes publishing a white paper to make the legal jurisdiction for Wales clearer and supports reform of the Barnett formula, it is silent on support for further powers for the Welsh Assembly. The Welsh Conservative Party has never adopted an official policy in favour of full legislative powers for the Assembly (Melding, 2012: 129). However, in the Welsh context, this ambivalence is certainly not confined to the Conservatives, with residual elements (essentially a number of MPs) in the Welsh Labour Party also sceptical about further devolution in the Government of Wales Act (Wyn Jones and Scully, 2011). Through its contribution to the St David's Day process, the Welsh Conservatives have outlined some distinctive positions in contrast to the UK Government's proposals. For instance, the leader of the Welsh Conservatives, Andrew R.T. Davies, openly opposed the 'lock-step' mechanism in the new financial powers that would have forced AMs to raise or lower all levels of tax at the same time.

Welshification and the nationalist card

The Welsh Conservative Party chose under the leadership of Nick Bourne to pursue a strategy of detoxifying the party's brand. However, unlike the UK Conservative Party under Cameron, this strategy related much more to issues of national identity. In a speech in 2005, Nick Bourne explicitly acknowledged his interpretation of this problem: 'Despite our pride in Welsh culture and heritage, and our Unionist credentials, Welsh Conservatives have been hindered by the notion that we are in some way an "English party". The idea that Conservatism is something imposed on Wales, not truly Welsh, has lingered for some time' (Bourne, 2005). Bourne also stresses the importance of the opposition parties working together in order to provide an alternative government for Wales that did not involve the Labour Party. It was therefore the explicit strategy of the Welsh Conservative Party to be in a realistic position to be in a coalition government in Wales (interview with AM 5, 2 March 2012).

As Melding (2012: 130) notes: 'Well before the 2007 election Nick Bourne launched a campaign to detoxify the party and make it a potential coalition partner with the Liberal Democrats and Plaid Cymru.' This manifested itself in the moderate tone of the party's manifestos and in the dropping of policies that the party had pursued under the Conservative Governments in Wales (1979–1997). The Mid- and West Wales Conservative AM Glyn Davies was absolutely clear in 2007 about the direction the party needed to take:

> I think it's absolutely essential that we as a Conservative Party are in the frame to be a part of a coalition. We've got to say to the people of Wales that we're a Welsh party; we want to be involved in the government of Wales … For anything other than a Labour-dominated government, it has to be a coalition between Plaid, the Conservatives and probably the Liberal Democrats as well. It doesn't work in any

other way – and maybe it doesn't work at all ... The challenge is for the Conservatives. At the moment there are a lot of people in Wales who think of the Conservatives as being an English party ... and we've got to change that perception ... There are a lot of people in Plaid Cymru who see the Tories as being beyond the pale. But there are a lot of people in Plaid for whom the Tories are very much the second choice as well. (Quoted in Shipton, 2011: 187–188)

Thus, the party in Wales rediscovered something of an office-seeking edge. Similarly, for one AM, the perceived existence of a soft Plaid Cymru vote made rebranding along nationalist lines essential:

I think we have certainly Welshified our brand, and I hate that term, but I think it's true that we have embraced devolution. We have parked our tanks on the nationalists' lawn in a sense, I think. And that's why I think we have been successful in attracting some people, soft Plaid voters over the years. I don't think that we have lurched to the left, I think that we've had sensible reasonable, rational policies here which are appropriate for Wales, but we are a centre-right party, we have always made that absolutely clear, and we will continue to be a centre-right party, but there are a lot of people out there who vote for Plaid Cymru who are centre-right and it's those people we need to attract and that's why I think it's important that we continue on this road of being proud to be Welsh Conservatives. (Interview with Conservative AM 3, 1 March 2012)

For another AM also, this did not involve a specific move to the left. However, it did involve a process of what he described as adjusting to specific Welsh needs (interview with AM 5, 2 March 2012).

However, this strategy is manifestly elite-driven and involved, if not bypassing the membership of the party, then certainly pushing them along a path that they would not otherwise have chosen. For one Conservative AM,

there wasn't systematic resistance to the leadership, apart from, you know, a few members felt perhaps it was diluting our Britishness, but they were very much minority voices. But I don't think you could portray it as the grassroots demanding for reforms in this way and wanting to establish a much more explicitly Welsh identity. But obviously the leadership strongly sense that that is the direction we have to travel in. And I think when you get a strong lead from the leadership, then most members feel comfortable with that. (Interview with Conservative AM 6, 2 March 2012)

Similarly, another AM concedes that the leadership of the party was a step ahead of the membership on issues of national identity (interview with AM 5, 2 March 2012). However, it is difficult to identify a vocal minority of members who acted as a break on change in this area.

Conclusion

In 1997, the Welsh Conservative Party had a difficult inheritance. As in Scotland, it lost all of its MPs and campaigned against devolution. However, by 2011 the party had changed its policies and strategy significantly in order to try to appear like it wholeheartedly embraced devolution and could be a potential partner in the government of Wales. The party gradually ditched policies from before 1997 and determined to shed its English image. Nevertheless, whilst it is important to acknowledge this change, it is equally important not to overstate it.

The formal autonomy of the Welsh Conservative Party is weak. The Welsh Party Board is not a powerful institution and David Cameron remains technically the leader of the Welsh Conservative Party. Moreover, the party in Wales relies on the UK party for funding and is much more fully integrated into the UK party than the Scottish Conservatives. The Welsh Conservatives did not gain any further formal autonomy after the initial reforms in 1998 that created the Welsh Board.

However, in this context a change of leadership became a key driver of change for the Welsh Conservatives. The transition from Rod Richards to Nick Bourne precipitated a gradual change in the party's strategy and policy positions. Nick Bourne drew on the work of colleagues like David Melding to reposition the Welsh Conservatives as a more authentically Welsh political party, despite its continuing organisational ties to the UK party. In this, the party leadership was aided by the considerable leeway given to it over devolved policy matters by the UK party. It is important in this context to study the enacted as well as the formal organisation of sub-state political parties. Party constitutions do not tell the whole story (Van Houten, 2009).

Somewhat counter-intuitively at first glance, the lack of formal organisational autonomy in fact aided the elite-driven strategy of 'Welshification'. Weak extra-parliamentary structures and the same centralised policy-making apparatus as the UK party meant that control over strategy and the manifesto was concentrated in a small group around the leader in the Welsh Assembly. The weak institutionalisation of the Welsh Conservative Party at the sub-state level meant that greater party change was possible (Panebianco, 1988: 261).

Another key driver of change was the prospect of being in government in Wales. The Welsh Conservative Party went some way to rediscovering the Conservatives' natural office-seeking instincts. Several crucial consequences flow from an explicit decision to do what it takes to be in a coalition government in the Welsh Assembly. It meant changing the party's policies and image so that it could be considered a viable partner for parties on the left (the Liberal Democrats) and on the nationalist left (Plaid Cymru).

However, whilst there has been a great deal of change on policy towards key public services under the Assembly's control, like health and education, there has been somewhat less overt change on the party's attitude towards the constitution. The party has never been formally in favour of legislative powers for the Welsh Assembly. During the 2011 referendum, the party could only agree to a neutral stance, although the majority of AMs campaigned for more powers and no AM explicitly campaigned against (Melding, 2012: 130).

Notes

1 Nicholas Edwards was created Lord Crickhowell in 1987.
2 Nicholas Edwards is consistently impressed with the influence of the Scottish Office, particularly under George Younger, to shut down tricky debates in cabinet and defend its position (Crickhowell, 1999: 53–61).
3 Mr Richards decided in 2013 to join the United Kingdom Independence Party (BBC News, 2013).
4 Two Conservative MSPs (interviews with Conservative MSPs 4 and 8) told the author that they were certain that Murdo Fraser could have won the 2011 leadership election if he had adopted a similar strategy. In 2001, it could also be argued that Portillo sought a mandate for radical change by being very clear about his intentions in a party that was probably not ready for it (Snowdon, 2010: 82).

5

Comparing party change in Scotland and Wales

I mean, the Welsh party has no autonomy at all. They have a bunch of volunteers who sit down called the Welsh Board who have no power at all; everything is decided in London. However, what they have been able to do through very good communication is create a strategy and develop a theme of Welsh autonomy and Welsh decision-making and that is the key thing we have needed to learn. (Interview with Scottish official 4, 30 November 2012)

We used to have quite a bit initially [contact with Scottish Conservatives]. And it was interesting how different many of their things were. I think we were always rather jealous of the fact that at that time they had, I will say a dozen, certainly something like that, working in Scottish Central Office, whereas we had four and one of those was part time. We were doing jolly well! (Interview with Conservative AM 1, 27 February 2012)

Introduction

Having examined party change in the cases of the Scottish and Welsh Conservative parties in detail, this chapter outlines a more focused comparison, drawing together the literature on sub-state parties and party change. The central conclusion is that the more substantial changes in the Welsh Conservative Party are explained broadly by the vision of the people in charge. People mattered a great deal more than party structures. Much like the UK Conservative Party, the Welsh and Scottish Conservative parties were vehicles that could be led.

This chapter begins by considering devolution and organisational change. The Scottish Conservative Party's structure was streamlined and expanded to accommodate the Scottish Parliament. More significantly, a Welsh Conservative Party was created for the first time. This chapter then compares the autonomy of the Welsh and Scottish Conservative parties. Both parties enjoyed a similarly strong measure of de facto autonomy from the UK Conservatives. This chapter then finds that leadership change had the potential to be significant for the Scottish Conservatives, but they decided not to seize the opportunity of the potential critical juncture of the 2011 leadership election. In contrast, the slow-burning effects of the transition from Rod Richards to Nick Bourne were crucial in its adaptation to devolution. The big change in the outlook of the Scottish Conservatives on devolution did not happen as a result of leadership change, but rather because of the external stimulus of the 2014 independence referendum and the danger to the Union that it posed.

This chapter then outlines an explanation for the differences in approach of the two parties through the prism of institutions, ideas and people. Finally, it considers the implications for the study of sub-state parties and concludes by discussing the idea of the definition of problems.

Devolution and party organisational change

A significant alteration of a party's institutional environment, like significant decentralisation within a state or the introduction of a new electoral system, may force a party to adapt if it wishes to remain relevant. However, whilst it is highly likely that this will result in change to a party's organisation, it is not at all guaranteed to make it change in any other way. Instead, for the Scottish and Welsh Conservatives, significant party change in other areas depended on those who had their hands on the levers of power.

Having been against devolution for so long, the external shock of the arrangements for the new Scottish Parliament and Welsh Assembly prompted some soul-searching for the sub-state Conservative Party. However, most obviously, it prompted organisational change in Scotland and Wales. This resulted in two highly autonomous branches of the statewide Conservative Party. In Scotland, a previously more separate structure was confirmed and put on a sounder institutional footing. In Wales, the beginnings of a separate party were created for the first time.

Changes in a party's institutional context drive change here in a manner we might expect. If a regional list element is added to the electoral system or a new regional legislature is created, then party organisational change is likely to occur (unless a party plans a principled boycott). Such processes took place in all of the UK's political parties after devolution (Fabre, 2008; Bratberg, 2009).

However, beyond creating new structures to 'fit' with the new institutions and proportional electoral systems, organisational change was not accompanied by change in other areas. In Scotland, this encumbered the party for the next decade with an organisational structure that was deliberately designed not to make the Scottish Parliament a priority. In Wales, the weak institutional structures accentuated the power of the party's leadership in the Welsh Assembly. Moreover, although these environmental changes were accompanied by leadership change (to the extent that new leadership positions were created), this did not initially have much impact. These changes took much longer to feed through the system, particularly in Wales. This is similar to the effect of Angela Merkel's leadership on the German CDU, where party change took a long time to be realised (Clemens, 2009: 135).

Devolution and sub-state party autonomy

The UK Conservative Party is, perhaps surprisingly, very accommodating of sub-state difference, provided it does not interfere with the party's priority of being in power at a UK level (Convery, 2014a). Thus, in Scotland and Wales, both parties had almost complete de facto autonomy over policy, leadership and candidate selection. However, both parties relied to a greater or lesser degree on funding from the statewide Conservative Party. Over the period of devolution, none of these indicators of autonomy changed significantly for either party.

In the Conservative Party, although power is dispersed to some extent at different levels, this arises from central party ignorance or benign neglect, rather than because it is particularly tolerant or welcoming of sub-state input into national decisions. Nor does it occur as a deliberate product of the way the party was formed or is structured. Moreover, in contrast to literature that suggests territorial party demands for autonomy, what is remarkable in the Conservative Party is the extent to which sub-national elites know and accept (perhaps even *embrace*) their place in a hierarchy that places a strong premium on Westminster office. In this sense, they embrace the statecraft goals of the centre. Access on a territorial basis to central policy-making is tokenistic and extremely limited, but this is not in the main resisted by the territorial branches.

In this sense, comparing the territorial Conservative Party to the party at an English level is like viewing the lopsided nature of devolution in the UK. While there has been considerable devolution to Scotland and Wales, England is still run as if it were a unitary state. In a similar fashion, the central Conservative Party's relationship with English constituency associations and area forums is in most respects much more explicitly hierarchical than its relationship with Scotland and Wales.

Leadership selection

In terms of leadership selection, both parties held contests without overt interference from the central party in the post-devolution period. Annabel Goldie was elected leader of the Scottish Conservatives without a contest and Ruth Davidson became leader in 2011 without any suggestion of UK party interference in the process. In 2011, no senior politician at the centre of the UK party questioned the Scottish Conservatives' right to break away entirely, and indeed Francis Maude, a former party chairman, had previously suggested such a plan.

Similarly, in Wales it is also difficult to detect any central party involvement in leadership selection. The UK party left the party to its own devices during the elections of Rod Richards, Nick Bourne and most recently, in 2011, Andrew R.T. Davies. The same cannot be said for the Labour Party in Wales. Under the reforms of the Sanderson Commission, the Scottish Conservative Party's leadership selection procedures became more democratic during the post-devolution period. This links with a general trend towards democratising leadership selection in political parties (Le Duc, 2001; Cross and Blais, 2012).

Candidate selection

Both parties also selected their candidates without overt interference from the central Conservative Party. The main difference is that whilst the Welsh party has to use the UK central candidates list for Westminster selections, Scotland has its own approved list. During some Scottish by-elections, particularly under Cameron's leadership, the UK party played a more prominent role, but this was in the main welcomed by the Scottish party.

Policy autonomy

The policy autonomy of the Welsh and Scottish Conservative parties over areas covered by the devolved administrations was almost absolute. No interviewee could point to any time where the central party vetoed a policy; nor did any admit to self-censorship in Scotland and Wales about policies they knew were implicitly off-limits. In the case of Wales, this has led to some significant policy divergence.

Finance

Both the Welsh and Scottish Conservative parties now rely on the statewide party for financial security. Both Conservative AM 6 (interview, 2 March 2012) and Conservative AM 1 (interview, 27 February 2012) were clear that separation for the Welsh Conservative Party would mean a significant drop in funding. Conservative AM 1 doubted the party could survive without support from the UK party. It does not exist as a separate entity and its fundraising capacity is limited.

In contrast, in Scotland, the financial situation pre-devolution and at the beginning of the Scottish Parliament was much healthier. In particular, donations from Lord Laidlaw allowed the party to spend a considerable amount on the 1999 Scottish Parliament elections.

Thus, the significance of the difference between what we might call a party's *formal* and *enacted* organisation is apparent. The constitution of the Welsh Conservative Party suggests only the most modest commitment to the creation of a separate territorial party. One Scottish party official is quite clear that, theoretically, 'the Welsh party has no autonomy at all. They have a bunch of volunteers who sit down called the Welsh Board who have no power at all; everything is decided in London' (interview with Scottish official 4, 30 November 2012). Instead, when we triangulate findings with party manifestos, speeches and in-depth interviews, we find that on all measures apart from finance, the Welsh Conservative Party enjoyed the same level of freedom as the Scottish Conservatives. Indeed, further, we find that while the Welsh Conservatives have pushed at the limits of their extremely limited party organisation, the Scottish party behaved as though it was not constitutionally separate at all. For Melding (2013: 43), the Scottish Conservative Party's 'culture has remained unitary, even ultra-unionist'. Thus, the behaviour of these parties was only dictated

Table 5.1 Indicators of autonomy for the Welsh and Scottish Conservatives

	Scotland		Wales	
	1999	2011	1999	2011
Leadership selection	Decentralised	Decentralised	Decentralised	Decentralised
Candidate selection	Decentralised	Decentralised	Decentralised*	Decentralised*
Policy-making	Decentralised	Decentralised	Decentralised but negotiated for some issues	Decentralised but negotiated for some issues
Finance	Considerable own resources	Raises money but controlled by UK party**	Reliant on UK party	Reliant on UK party

* Westminster candidates must be chosen from the UK approved list.
** Under the terms of the Sanderson reforms in 2010, the party raises money in Scotland and remits it to the UK party. The UK party then gives a share back to Scotland. A party official said that this gave the Scottish party financial security and that the Scottish party still met its own costs (interview with Scottish official 4, 30 November 2012).

by party organisation to a very limited extent: instead, in the flexible Conservative Party, the limits on Wales and Scotland's room for manoeuvre were in the hands of a UK leadership whose attention was mainly elsewhere (see, for instance, Bale, 2010).

However, it is by no means inevitable that statewide parties grant such strong autonomy to sub-state branches. The contrast with the Spanish statewide parties, for instance, is quite stark. Detterbeck (2012) notes that the branches of the Spanish PSOE and PP do not possess the same autonomy as the Welsh and Scottish Conservatives. The Scottish Labour Party's struggle with integration and autonomy continues and former leader Johann Lamont recently described how she felt like she was in charge of a 'branch office' (*Daily Record*, 2014).

Leadership and faction change

As Bale (2010: 17) points out: 'A change of leadership in the Conservative Party is, in effect, regime change.' This is also the case in the territorial branches of the Conservative Party. Power lies in the party leadership, rather than at conferences or at a constituency level. Moreover, at root the political culture of the Conservative Party is one that wants to be led. For one Scottish party official: 'I think loyalty is a big, big thing within the Conservative Party' (interview with Scottish official 1, 25 October 2011). Another commented on how far Conservative members could be pushed in terms of supporting further fiscal devolution to Scotland:

I mean, what I would say is, in terms of the feeling of the Party ... Conservatives are quite hierarchical, very hierarchical, and they are loyal and they will take quite a lot. I mean that's what David Cameron found, as long as they believe they are going to win, that's what they want at the end of the day, so you have to really push them to get them to move against the leadership, so as in most policy areas, I think that would have been, I think anything would have been acceptable. (Interview with Scottish official 4, 30 November 2012)

Similarly, Hayton (2012) concludes that David Cameron has been able to lead the Conservative Party away from some of its default tendencies and towards a more electable image and policy platform. Thus, leadership change in any part of the Conservative Party offers substantial scope for party change because internal democracy is weak and because of a desire to win which temporarily suppresses other considerations (Ramsden, 1998; Ball, 2005).

However, although these very powerful levers were available to successive leaders of the Conservative Party in Scotland, none elected to use them. In the case of David McLetchie, the existence of a section of the party (particularly in the membership) that remained at best uneasy and at worst hostile to devolution meant that he felt unable to move the party forward on this issue. Instead, the Scottish Conservative Party became under his leadership a competent opposition party in a multi-party Parliament. To the extent that none of the MSPs were actively hostile to devolution and threw themselves into the work of the Parliament and its committees, the Scottish Conservative Party had come to terms with devolution (see, for instance, Douglas-Hamilton, 2009, chapter 13). However, no substantial new initiatives were taken regarding policies, national identity or dealing with what might be wrong with the party's brand in Scotland. McLetchie did not apparently consider these to be the main problem.

Similarly, under the leadership of Annabel Goldie, the priority was not to deal with issues of national identity, brand or a major policy rethink. Instead, she prioritised the selling of the idea that the Scottish Conservatives were relevant and that they could deliver. This led indirectly to the Conservatives being able to work very well with the SNP minority administration in passing three out of its four budgets.

Both leaders had more autonomy from the central party than they needed or wanted to be able to achieve these goals. Instead, the lack of change in the Scottish Conservative Party is best explained by a lack of desire to change. The rejection of Murdo Fraser during the 2011 leadership election also reflected the lack of appetite within the party membership for a radical overhaul. They instead found comfort in the implementation of the previously agreed organisational reforms recommended by Lord Sanderson's commission. Their interpretation of the Scottish Conservative Party's problem was, therefore, not the message or the brand, but its ineffective communication.

In contrast, in Wales, the transition from the leadership of Rod Richards to Nick Bourne marked a decisive shift in the party's strategy in the medium and long term. He had a fundamentally different conception of the 'problems' of the Welsh Conservative Party. The greatest barrier to their full integration into the Welsh political system was both their policy positions and their national identity. Thus, under his leadership, the Conservatives significantly changed their policy stance and concentrated on appearing as champions for Wales. The difference between the 1999 manifesto and those of 2003, 2007 and 2011 is stark.

Bourne's programme of change was helped by a significant faction within the Welsh Conservative Party that shared his vision for the future. In particular, David Melding provided the intellectual basis for such a shift in strategy and was in charge of the drafting of the party's manifestos. This strategy was an elite-driven project that went ahead of the membership (interview with Conservative AM 5, 2 March 2012). However, unlike in Scotland, the party leadership did not see such attitudes or an anti-devolution feeling in the party as impeding their agenda. This may be due to the weaker institutionalisation of the Welsh Conservative Party. The lack of a powerful Central Office (which had existed in Scotland for years and was retained under the Strathclyde reforms) and the installation of a relatively weak Welsh Party Board meant that there were fewer institutional constraints for the party leadership in the Assembly. Thus, armed with the same de facto policy autonomy as the Scottish party, a leader with a clear strategy for change in Wales was able to significantly alter the party's policy programme. All AMs interviewed for this study credited Nick Bourne for this strategy and, in particular, the idea of appearing 'more Welsh' or 'Welshification' (interview with Conservative AM 3, 1 March 2012).

Thus, in post-devolution Scotland and Wales, ideological factional arguments on a left-right scale did not really exist. Instead, in the Conservative Party, the main splits were over devolution itself. In Wales, the change of leadership from Rod Richards to Nick Bourne ensured a new faction took charge that embraced devolution and pursued a new specifically Welsh profile for the party. Leadership and factional change is the main driver for other changes in the party. In contrast, in Scotland, there was not until the 2011 leadership election a vocal or visible faction within the party that was alive to the Conservative possibilities of devolution. Instead, David McLetchie and Annabel Goldie chose not to confront a significant body of opinion within the party that expressed only grudging support for devolution. Both leaders did not set much store by the ideas of brand detoxification or that their policies were outside the mainstream. Thus, whilst the Welsh Conservative Party concentrated on problems at a macro level (the system-wide perceptions of the party that they thought prevented voters from engaging with its message), in Scotland leaders concentrated instead on micro (on-the-ground campaigning) and meso (institutional organisation) level problems that were easier, both intellectually and practically, to resolve.

Constitutional changes, electoral defeat and (further) organisational change in Scotland and Wales

The main change prompted by the initial introduction of devolution for both parties was in terms of organisation. For both parties, this constitutional change also came almost directly after one of the Conservative Party's worst ever election defeats. For the Welsh Conservatives, organisation has remained largely constant since the original Welsh Party Board was created in 1998. For the Scottish Conservatives, the Strathclyde reforms of 1998 were much more wide-ranging. However, whilst they also had consequences for internal party debates and disagreements, post-devolution leaders felt that they were inconvenienced rather than significantly constrained by the structures Strathclyde created.

Just as significant in terms of organisational reform for the Scottish Conservatives was the defeat in 2010 as well as in 1997. This caused a similar level of trauma as the 1997 defeat. Using Janda *et al.*'s (1995: 182–183) classifications of party defeats, 2010 may be placed alongside 1997 as not merely 'disappointing' but 'calamitous'. Indeed, one party official thinks that it created a unique potential critical juncture for radical party change that was not seized:

> I think if the leadership election had been in 2010, then Murdo [Fraser] would have won ... Because that is the biggest point that there has been palpable ... amongst people who have done it all, been through it all, been at the counts, lost everything, lost whatever, you know, just thought, oh shit ... we have got a Tory prime minister again and we have made no progress here. So I think it took that because I think 2005, because of Michael Howard, people didn't really ... a lot of people didn't like him ... 2001 you could say, William Hague, that's why we didn't do well and Labour had been returned at Westminster, therefore of course Scotland is going to vote Labour. It took until 2010 to realise, well, actually, there is something more fundamental wrong. (Interview with Scottish official 4, 30 November 2012)

Thus, in Panebianco's terms, this defeat resulted in a crisis of identity and legitimacy for the party's dominant elites who appeared to have lost control over the key 'zones of uncertainty' (Panebianco, 1988: 246). Thus: 'the full support given by the believers in exchange for symbolic remuneration (namely, the tutelage of collective identity) is withdrawn. The specific consensus the careerists gave in return for material remuneration and/or status is also withdrawn' (Panebianco, 1988: 246).

However, the response to such a defeat was organisational rather than ideological: the establishment of the Sanderson Commission. Subsequently, the party rejected the radical proposals of Murdo Fraser at the 2011 leadership election for more thoroughgoing change. The period of flux and crisis of legitimacy may have settled by 2011 and reduced the willingness of party members to embark on the 'adventure' proposed by an alternative to the dominant elites in the party (Panebianco, 1988: 246).

A tale of two parties? Institutions, ideas and people in Scotland and Wales

How did a Welsh party with almost no autonomy on paper end up changing more and becoming more territorially distinctive than a Scottish counterpart with considerably more power and freedom? By combining previous scholarship about party change and sub-state parties with detailed interviews and documentary analysis, this study builds an explanation through three themes: institutions, ideas and people.

First, in terms of institutions, the Welsh nation and the Scottish nation, and consequently the Welsh Assembly and the Scottish Parliament, are entirely different projects at varying stages of maturity. From the outset, the Scottish Parliament was an institution at the harder end of a federal spectrum that represented a stateless nation. In Wales, the Welsh Assembly reflected an uneasy compromise (mostly as a result of internal arguments in the Labour Party) between those who saw Wales as a nation and those who did not. Thus, a path to being seen to accept and embrace devolution was much clearer for the Welsh Conservatives. From almost every political perspective, the design of the 1999 Welsh Assembly was deeply unsatisfactory and presented opportunities to suggest improvements that could not easily be branded as concessions to nationalists (Melding, 2012). In Scotland, there was not a great deal of scope to strengthen the Scottish Parliament, beyond proposing greater fiscal devolution,[1] which was more difficult because it was complicated and appeared more radical.

Second, in such a context, some in the Welsh party began to think differently about the possibilities of devolution. Thinkers within the party started to articulate the idea of an authentically Welsh Conservative agenda (Evans, 2002; Melding, 2001, 2009; Bourne, 2005). Such an effort is comparable with some of the thinking that underpinned the Cameron modernisation agenda in the UK Conservative Party (for instance, Vaizey et al., 2001; Boles, 2010). In Scotland, there was not only a dearth of new ideas, but also a lack of interest in pursuing any of them. Instead, the party chose the easier and achievable task of integrating itself in the Scottish Parliament, becoming a competent opposition party. The party was so successful in this endeavour that it was able to work well with the SNP minority government, 2007–2011, to pass three of its budgets and achieve some concessions on business rates, town centre regeneration and police numbers. However, in terms of party change, this was displacement activity. It did not address more fundamental questions about the future of Scottish Conservatism (Smith, 2011).

Nevertheless, such differences in institutional and party organisational conditions are not sufficient to fully explain party change. Third, and crucially in the hierarchical Conservative Party, the Welsh Conservatives had elected members who shared the analysis and goals of revisionist thinkers within the party. Thus, while a change of leadership in Scotland made almost no difference to party strategy, the transition from Rod Richards to Nick Bourne represented a fundamental shift in

Table 5.2 Conservative Party change in Scotland and Wales, 1997–2011

	Personnel	Organisation	Policy	Autonomy
Scotland	Limited	Significant	None to limited	None
Wales	Moderate	None	Significant	None

how the Welsh Conservatives formulated policy and presented themselves. In contrast, in her 2013 speech to the Scottish Conservative Party conference in Stirling, Ruth Davidson was still proposing essentially the same version of school vouchers trailed in the Rifkind Policy Commission in 1998.

For Hayton (2012), David Cameron's reconstruction of Conservatism did not amount to much more than putting a more appealing gloss on policies that were still constrained by a neo-Thatcherite inheritance. In Wales, it could be argued that the reconstruction of Conservatism has gone much further towards a One Nation tradition (Hayton, 2012: 28–31).

Sub-state party change

In the Conservative Party, leadership change can be decisive for party change because it is a party with weak internal democracy and a hierarchical culture. This study has found that broadly the same assumption holds in its sub-state branches. Internal democracy and members' input into policy-making is no greater in Scotland and Wales than it is at the UK level. Substantive decisions are not taken at party conferences; they are taken by a small group around the party leader.

In terms of sub-state parties, it is worth reflecting that the default setting for these parties need not always to demand more autonomy for the region and the party. We should not assume that sub-state parties are always straining at the leash. Instead, we have to examine the particular motivations of sub-state elites and at what level they would most like their party to be in power. Second, examining the formal organisational autonomy of a sub-state party will not always tell us how much room for manoeuvre it has in practice. Party constitutions are not living documents. They tend only to come to life during moments of crisis (deselecting candidates) or when they are being changed (during the Strathclyde and Sanderson Commissions). Otherwise, they remain in the drawer and of interest only to party officials and political scientists. Thus, party autonomy may in part, as Van Houten (2009) suggests, only become explicitly apparent during moments of crisis. However, we can use other methods such as interviews and examination of documents and speeches to gauge the extent to which sub-national parties can change their policy programmes or choose candidates.

A party's *formal* structures and arrangements for sub-state autonomy and its constitution are important as an expression of its attitude to territorial politics. However, it is also just as important to engage in detailed qualitative studies of a party's *enacted* organisation: what actually happens on the ground when the exact provisions of the constitution have been long forgotten by those busily engaged in everyday parliamentary politics and campaigning.

Conclusion: the construction of problems

Much depends on how problems are constructed. The Scottish Conservatives constructed their problems at the micro level: the problem is one of not having the right type of candidates or those candidates not working hard enough to communicate the party's message. The Welsh Conservatives saw their problems at a macro level: the problem is the brand of Welsh Conservatism. Until this was dealt with, party elites felt that the party could not move forward. Crucially, the Welsh Conservative Party's leadership decided that it wanted to be in power. The only route to power involved being a coalition partner with the two other left-leaning parties who had a history of loathing the Conservatives. Having made such a decision, the strategy that needs to be followed becomes much clearer. Being office-seeking in Wales requires a different set of calculations from being office-seeking at a UK level. Making this intellectual leap was crucial for Welsh Conservative elites.

Detterbeck and Hepburn (2010: 117) suggest that the Conservative Party adopted an autonomist strategy because there were elements in the Scottish and Welsh Conservative parties that desired further autonomy. Perhaps a more plausible explanation is that UK party elites were prepared to offer a high degree of self-rule for these parties because they could have no negative impact on the party's primary goal of securing office at Westminster. Thus, there may very well have been elements in the Scottish and Welsh Conservative parties that desired more autonomy, but this was not the primary reason why it was granted. Indeed, this study argues that the Scottish Conservatives in fact had *more* autonomy than they needed or wanted. The UK party did not pursue an assimilationist strategy with regard to Scotland: on the contrary, the *Scottish* Conservative Party did.

Note

1 Although Murdo Fraser proposed this in a pamphlet entitled *Full Fiscal Autonomy* in 1998 (before his election to the Scottish Parliament), he did not take up this theme again until his leadership election campaign in 2011.

PART III

Conclusion

Devolution, party politics and conservatism

This book began with the puzzle of the contrasting fortunes of the Welsh and Scottish Conservative parties. Through a comparative examination of party change it sought to find out *how* but also, crucially, *why* both parties changed in the way they did after devolution. Using an analytical framework derived from the literature on party change and multi-level party politics, it explored the reactions of both parties on a series of common drivers and indicators of change.

This conclusion draws together the two strands of party change and the sub-state Conservative Party that have run through this book. It begins with conclusions about the Conservative Party itself. It then considers what this case suggests about the wider study of multi-level party politics.

A tale of two parties

The Welsh and Scottish Conservative parties both faced similar challenges in different contexts in 1997. The Welsh Conservatives were able, despite their lack of formal autonomy, to more successfully manage four central post-devolution challenges: being a statewide party in a sub-state context; finding a party goal or new sense of purpose; making sense of the Thatcher legacy and the Conservative Governments (1979–1990); and dealing with devolution.

First, both parties had to work out how to be effective statewide parties in sub-state contexts. They had to find a way of appearing to place Scotland and Wales first, whilst also maintaining their commitment to the integrity of the UK. This is the essential tension for statewide parties (Roller and Van Houten, 2003). The Welsh Conservatives managed to do this by realising that constantly emphasising a Conservative commitment to the UK was not necessary. The Scottish Conservatives could not break out of the priority of Westminster office. While the Welsh Conservatives saw a need to try to appear as distinctly Welsh as possible, the Scottish Conservatives happily stuck more closely to the UK party.

Second, in the absence of the previous UK office-seeking priority, both parties had to find a new sense of purpose or mission. The Scottish Conservatives concentrated their energy on being a competent opposition party in a multi-party parliament and, especially at the 2011 elections, tailored their manifesto to emphasise how they could be relevant by winning concessions from the Government. The Conservatives in Scotland could not (or would not) envisage a path to being in government in the Scottish Parliament. In contrast, the Welsh Conservatives under Nick Bourne rediscovered an appetite for power and could see a path to achieving it. Significant consequences flow from a desire to do what it takes to be in power in the Welsh Assembly. This laid out a clear path for dealing with both Thatcherism and devolution.

In terms of making sense of the legacy of Thatcherism and the Conservative Governments (1979–1997), the Scottish Conservatives found it difficult in many areas to move on from policies they had pursued in government before 1997. They lacked an incentive to fundamentally re-examine their policy platform because they were not in search of new voters or a plausible programme for coalition government. Their main strategy was to attract back voters who identified as Conservatives but did not vote for the party. In contrast, for the Welsh Conservatives under Nick Bourne, there was a deliberate strategy to deal with the legacy of the Conservative Governments and previous opposition to devolution. From the 2003 manifesto, they began to abandon or repackage older policies and present themselves wherever possible in a distinctly Welsh manner. This is the difference between the Scottish Conservatives' pragmatic acceptance of devolution and the Welsh Conservatives' imaginative embrace. Without the external shock of the 2014 independence referendum, there is little to suggest that the Scottish Conservatives would have so decisively altered their attitude on devolution, having elected a leader who declared that the Calman Commission was a 'line in the sand'.

Losing an empire, finding a goal

The British state has been a principal cast member in this study. The peculiar workings of administrative devolution created strange incentives and dulled consequences for the Conservatives. It was not necessary to win a majority of seats or votes in Scotland and Wales in order to govern. This is also the case of course in England. However, when the plurinational element of the UK is taken into consideration alongside administrative devolution, this has consequences that go beyond those in, for instance, the difference in voting patterns between the north and south of England. The Conservatives were artificially sustained in office in Scotland and Wales. This not only had lethal consequences for their electoral success; it also trapped many of them in a warped sense of what was possible or implementable without power flowing through Westminster and without a severely majoritarian electoral system.

To be clear, there is nothing about the British Constitution that suggests governing different parts of the UK is illegitimate or lacks a mandate if it is not accompanied by a majority of votes or seats in that region.[1] However, declining Conservative Party support in both Scotland and Wales in the 1980s and 1990s[2] combined with administrative devolution created the impression that it was governing beyond or at the limits of its authority. Opposition to the Conservative Party mobilised the base of support for the Scottish Parliament in 1997.

Thus, adding a democratic element to administrative devolution fundamentally shifted the political and policy possibilities. The economic shift rightwards of the Conservative Party in Scotland in the 1980s (Seawright, 1999), for example, did not have electoral consequences that removed the Conservatives from the Scottish Office. They were thus able to pursue assimilationist policies in health and education that were beyond what might be considered as mainstream policy-making. This manifested itself in, for instance, nursery vouchers in Wales and grant-maintained schools in Scotland.

In the post devolution period, it became difficult to shake off this inheritance. The Scottish Conservatives broadly stuck to the same themes in health and education for the next decade and more. However, the Welsh Conservatives managed to move on more comprehensively because key party elites decided that they wanted to be in government. The Welsh Conservatives needed therefore to make themselves a viable coalition partner for two other parties of the centre-left. David Melding is quite clear, for instance, about the idea of placing the Welsh Conservatives on the 'optimum centre-right position of the *Welsh* political spectrum', not the centre-right of England or the UK (Melding, 2012: 176). In contrast, the Scottish Conservatives could never make the mental leap necessary in order to explicitly locate the party on what might be considered the moderate centre-right of Scottish politics (where many SNP members might be located: see, for instance, MacLeod and Russell, 2006). In the absence of the explicit goal of office, they diligently applied themselves to being a respectable opposition party in the parliament: a process that might be called 'banal parliamentarianism'. This mirrored processes that Alexander Smith (2011) observed in his ethnographic study of the Conservative Party in Dumfries: banal activism in place of a strategy.

However, even before 1999, the Conservatives failed to recognise that they were buffeting against the acceptable limits of administrative devolution: both for the party itself and the Welsh and Scottish nations. Would it seriously have been satisfactory for the Conservative Party to continue to govern Scotland and Wales with a dwindling number of MPs? John Major hints that he could foresee the inevitability of devolution in the mid-1990s, but he could not take such a thought to its logical conclusion for the Conservative Party.

The party was also hitting against one of the paradoxes of appealing to Scottish or Welsh aspirations through its form of devolution. Granting more powers to the Scottish or Welsh Offices meant that they could sometimes be seen as even more illegitimate because they were now being exercised by a government of Scotland or Wales that lacked strong political support. Latterly, Michael Forsyth tried to deal with this by devolving power even further towards Scottish local authorities. However, according to one Scottish official, it was by then too late (interview with Scottish official 2, 2 November 2011).

This study has identified three central factors that eased the Welsh Conservatives' transition, but which were not present to the same extent in Scotland. First, there was the different context of devolution. The powers and standing orders of the first Welsh Assembly were almost universally considered inadequate. This provided an opportunity from the outset for the Conservatives to be on board with the devolution project in a manner that did not seem to hard-line supporters like it involved making concessions to Plaid Cymru. The Conservatives were then able to publicly demonstrate their commitment to devolution when all senior members of the Welsh party campaigned for a Yes vote in the 2011 referendum. The substantial initial powers of the Scottish Parliament, forged in large measure through the consensus of the Scottish Constitutional Convention, did not afford the Scottish Conservatives this opening.

Second, the nature of the Welsh party system means that any alternative to the Labour Party being in government in Wales has to involve the Conservative Party. In contrast, in Scotland, the greater strength of the SNP presents the possibility of governing coalitions or minorities that do not need to involve the Conservatives. The Conservatives' pivotal position in Wales places some responsibility upon party elites who believe strongly that Wales should have an alternative to Labour in government. In Scotland, the Conservatives can be more painlessly ignored.

Third, the post-devolution Welsh Conservative Party was much more weakly institutionalised than the Scottish Conservative Party (Panebianco, 1988: 261). This presented party elites with an opportunity to change the party that involved consulting or bypassing fewer party activists or officials with their own power base. In the words of a party official, 'policy development happens in this [National Assembly] building' (interview with Welsh official, 26 March 2013). The Welsh Central Office is weak and does not have the same history of autonomy as the Scottish party's central office.

However, alongside these more favourable circumstances for party change, the Welsh Conservatives had politicians within the pool of its AMs who were determined to change the party. Nick Bourne was able to take advantage of the above circumstances, but, crucially, people who thought like him and David Melding had to be selected as candidates in the first place. We return therefore to Harmel and Janda's (1994) un-improvable observation that party change does not 'just happen'. The crucial intervening variable between changing circumstances and party change is how problems are perceived and constructed by those in charge. Significant party change requires those determined to carry it out to be available to take up leadership positions.

The Conservative Party

In his resignation letter to Gordon Brown in 2009, James Purnell wrote: 'We both love the Labour Party ... We know we owe it everything and it owes us nothing.' As Robin Harris (2011: 4) argues, 'No Conservative politician at any stage of the party's history would have written such a letter'. The Conservative Party has instead been viewed by scholars as having instrumental value, rather than a sense of attachment for its own sake (for instance, Blake, 1985; Davies, 1995; Norton, 1996: 10; Ramsden, 1998; Ball, 2005). As Norton (1996: 2) observes, 'Conservatives are not prone to reflect on why they are as they are ... they are more concerned with the practicalities of life and learning from experience, than they are with abstract reasoning and reflection'. The often-implicit idea that the pursuit of office is the primary function of the Conservative Party is a feature of its twentieth-century history.

Devolution thus presented Conservatives with a problem. Adding a democratic element to administrative devolution required it to become a different party in Scotland and Wales. This is especially the case because both the Scottish Parliament and the Welsh Assembly adopted proportional electoral systems. The Welsh Conservatives have shown that the Conservative Party can adapt to such a situation. However, it appears from this case study that the Conservative Party works best when there is the prospect of office. Change may be more likely when there is the prospect of office (Bale, 2012: 145). One of David Cameron's slogans during his leadership election campaign was 'Change to Win'. Murdo Fraser's campaign in 2011 reflects in part a rediscovery of the perceived instincts of the twentieth-century Conservative Party. If the objective is to win and the party is holding politicians back from winning, then the party has to go. It is difficult to think of a precedent for such a radical plan or of another UK party so equally lacking in sentimentality in which it could be contemplated.

It might be putting the case too strongly to suggest that there is no point in the Conservative Party unless it is seeking office (see, for instance, Harris, 2011: 4). However, it might be fairer to say that the Conservative Party works optimally, and its elites are able fully to take advantage of its flexible structures, when change can be justified on the basis that it is the only way to regain office. The Conservative Party may well have a distinctive purpose beyond this, but the Scottish Conservatives never appeared to manage to discover it.

The future of unionism in the Conservative Party rests now on the success of the further self-rule powers that the Cameron Government plans to devolve to Scotland and Wales. The centre of the Conservative Party has shown little or no interest in sub-state Conservatives' thoughts about the renewal of unionism through the creation of an explicitly federal United Kingdom (see Melding, 2009). It has also largely ignored ideas about the creation of a Charter of Union (for instance, Bingham Centre for the Rule of Law, 2015). The party has no plans to change the centre of the UK state in order to accommodate devolution (other than through English Votes for English Laws). Its commitment to the Union is thus a lopsided one. There is no doubt that, for example, the leadership of the Conservative Party, in particular David Cameron, 'gets' Scotland insofar as it has moved on substantively from the party's attitudes to devolution in the 1990s. Cameron has a thoroughly pragmatic approach and has embraced further devolution as an example of decentralisation and the application of the Conservative principle of political responsibility. In the 1990s the party might have been accused of concentrating on enhancing Scottish representation and input into UK-wide decisions, whilst ignoring demands for Scottish self-rule. Now, arguably the opposite is the case: further substantial powers are being devolved to Scotland and Wales while the mechanics of the centre of the UK state remain unchanged.

What binds Scotland into the United Kingdom? Can an MP representing a Scottish seat ever again become Prime Minister of the United Kingdom? The Conservative Party is content to park these difficult questions and concentrate instead on giving Scotland what it thinks it wants. Unionism is important to the Conservative Party, but it is difficult to consider wide-ranging changes to the Westminster model and the centre of British government when you can achieve a majority without Scotland. If, however, the price of the Union becomes substantial and formalised devolved input into UK Government decisions, then we will find out how deep the party's unionism runs.

The drivers of party change

In light of this case study, we can make some observations about the nature of the drivers of party change. Defeat does not always drive party change. In particular, in multi-level states, *relative* electoral success between regions becomes important. Thus, whilst the UK Conservative Party performed poorly, the pressure on its Scottish branch to change was lessened, even though it made little progress. The pressure to change intensified only when the Welsh and UK parties started to outperform the Scottish Conservatives. Instead, in keeping with Deschouwer's (1992: 17) and Wilson's (1994) findings, what matters is how electoral defeat is *interpreted*. While decline could be blamed on a wider malaise within UK conservatism, the potential driver of electoral defeat was blunted. For the Welsh Conservatives, electoral defeat was not the main driver of party change. Thus, as Bale (2012: 316) concludes, 'election defeat is another example of a variable whose impact (and whose status) we should never simply assume'.

Where defeat did act as a driver of change, it tended to result in organisational changes, rather than shifts in policy or strategy. Both parties were reorganised in 1998 in response to the results of the 1997 general election and the implementation of devolution. The Scottish Conservatives also carried out another internal restructuring exercise in 2011 through the Sanderson reforms, prompted by their interpretation of the results of the 2010 general election in Scotland.

This case confirms Harmel et al.'s (1995: 6) finding that changes of leader may be necessary but not sufficient drivers of change. In the case of the Scottish Conservatives, one change of leadership (McLetchie to Goldie) occurred without any significant change in the party's organisation, strategy or policies. Similarly, Ruth Davidson's leadership was not in itself a catalyst for policy change. For the Welsh Conservatives, significant party change occurred when a change of leadership (Richards to Bourne) was also accompanied by a change in the party's dominant faction.

However, the evidence in this study does not support Harmel et al.'s (1995: 7) hypothesis that 'the relationship between leadership changes and party change is stronger for parties with strong leadership structures than for parties with severely limited leaders'. Instead, we must treat the variable of the power of party leadership much more cautiously, even in parties like the Conservative Party where a great deal of power (particularly in opposition) is placed in the hands of the leadership. Having significant powers to change a party is different from using them. Strong leadership structures provide the potential for change, but they do not necessarily make it more likely to happen. Thus, although the Scottish Conservatives were in Schumacher et al.'s (2013) terms dominated by the leadership and had few veto players, this party organisation did not lead them to respond more emphatically to environmental incentives.

Whilst there was no change in the dominant faction in charge of the Scottish Conservatives, the transition from Richards to Bourne in Wales did result in a shift in the party's dominant faction. Thus, for the Welsh Conservatives, party change followed factional change, as hypothesised by Harmel and Tan (2003). The impact of these drivers of change is not always immediate. As Clemens (2009) discovered for the German CDU under Merkel's leadership, changes can be inconsistent and ad hoc. The Welsh Conservatives under Nick Bourne began a gradual process of change, which, while significant in most areas, did not ever achieve a fully united policy for the party on further devolution.

An important driver of change present in Wales but absent in Scotland was the prospect of office. Thus, the political opportunity structure matters, particularly for parties that have traditionally been office-seeking. The opportunity to be in office in Wales was a central factor in the substantial changes in policy and presentation for the Welsh Conservatives. This gave the party a goal and a plan: holding office in Wales meant doing what it took to be a viable coalition partner for two parties of the centre-left.

Party change and multi-level politics

For the wider study of multi-level party politics, this study suggests four broad conclusions. First, there can be a marked difference between a party's *formal* organisation and its *enacted* organisation. In particular, it is not possible to divine the true extent of a sub-state party's autonomy by simply examining its constitutional structures. If we want to understand the extent of a sub-state party's autonomy on the ground, then it is necessary to engage with party elites about the informal 'everyday life' of political parties, which may at the sub-state level involve negotiation, conflict or indifference. On paper, the Scottish Conservative Party has more autonomy than the Welsh Conservative Party. In practice, both had similar levels of freedom and, somewhat counter-intuitively, the Welsh Conservatives ended up becoming more distinctive than their Scottish colleagues. Not having formal autonomy is not necessarily an indication of sub-state party subservience; having formal autonomy is different from using it.

Second, in this context, people seem to matter more than (formal) structures. In parties whose leaders can only be drawn from elected MPs, the extent of the thinking among them will in large measure determine the extent of party change. In parties like the Conservative Party with virtually no internal democracy (beyond leadership and candidate selection) this is especially important. The Conservative Party's sub-state branches mirror the flexibility of the UK organisation. Changes in leadership in Scotland and Wales also resemble wholesale changes in regime (Norton and Aughey, 1981: 266–267; Bale, 2010: 17). Thus, this case supports Fabre's (2008) central conclusion that parties' internal workings and leadership are crucial intervening variables in processes of sub-state adaptation. Parties do not simply respond to functional pressures (Bratberg, 2009).

Third, this case has demonstrated that the default setting for sub-state parties need not always be to demand more autonomy. Making this assumption for all sub-state parties has the potential to miss important subtleties in elites' loyalties and priorities. In particular, parties may choose to pursue an explicitly assimilationist strategy at the sub-state level because they perceive a higher level as the most important level of government. This study also found no evidence of factional conflict between the different levels of the Conservative Party.

Fourth, as predicted by Hopkin (2009: 228), sub-state parties exhibit features of institutional stickiness and path dependency. The Scottish Conservatives came to rely on a stock of policies and answers that served them in the 1980s and 1990s. In the post-devolution period, they found it extremely difficult to break out of this inheritance. They also had difficulty letting go of their traditional attachment to the priority of achieving office at the UK level. Whilst this was once a rational reaction to the political opportunity structure of the pre-devolution UK, after the creation of the Scottish Parliament it locked the party into a strategy that was increasingly sub-optimal.

Statewide parties and decentralisation

This conclusions presented here also suggest wider questions about what it means to be a statewide party in a plurinational and quasi-federal state. Does supporting more powers for the devolved legislatures necessarily involve a dilution of one's commitment to the central state? Is it impossible to remain a committed unionist whilst supporting greater policy divergence and perhaps an entirely separate sub-state party structure? The Sanderson Commission (2010) seemed to conclude that this was indeed the case. However, perhaps unexpectedly, the Conservative Party has come further in raising ideas in this area than any other UK statewide party.

Murdo Fraser's suggestion of an entirely separate party of the centre-right in Scotland goes further than any of the other statewide parties have thus far contemplated. In the end, the Conservatives in Scotland still held on to a view of a statewide party that was more unitary: that Scottish people should have the opportunity to vote for Conservative candidates. History may judge that, electorally, this was a noble act of self-sacrifice for a conception of unionism and being a statewide party that is increasingly challenged by the deepening of sub-state identity, policy divergence and party politics. For most Conservatives in Scotland in the 2011 leadership election, it appeared that unionism was, once again, an 'important matter of principle' (Seawright, 1999). Similarly, the strategy of the Welsh Conservative Party under Nick Bourne is more explicitly regionalist than the other statewide parties. The Welsh Conservatives have managed an under-the-radar transformation, but they lack the party structures to take what appears to be a logical step to becoming a fully Welsh political party. The greater threat to the Union surely lies in continued relative Conservative weakness in Scotland and Wales, rather than in a possible slide towards a Belgian-style break-up of statewide party links.

For a long time centre-right instincts allowed Conservatives to come some of the way towards a more radical position. Ian Lang, for instance, argued that devolution has created 'a supplicant and dependent Parliament – a sure recipe for the politics of grievance and the fostering of a dependency culture' (Lang, 2002: 192). A conception of unionism prevented him and others, however, from taking a step towards supporting a more fiscally powerful parliament or a more explicitly federal UK. It also appeared to stop the Conservatives in 2011 from taking the step towards being a separate political party. If a parliament dependent on resources and support from London has created a 'supplicant and dependent' institution, then surely the same arguments can be applied to the Scottish Conservative Party?

For Michael Russell (formerly the SNP Government's education secretary) and Dennis MacLeod (2006: 130), 'The Tories' problem is that their Unionist ideology is overcoming their free market common sense.' Until the endorsement of the Strathclyde Commission (2014) proposals for further devolution, and their explicit statement on the compatibility of unionism and (economic) conservatism, the Scottish Conservatives struggled to make sense of the tensions between these two ideologies (Mitchell and Convery, 2012).

This study has presented an analysis of the territorial Conservative Party through the wider comparative lenses of party change and multi-level party politics. The Scottish and Welsh Conservatives are not unique in facing the dilemmas of being statewide parties in regional contexts. Many other European parties of the centre-right must also confront multi-level politics. However, the nature of the British state and the Conservatives' place within it has deeply marked their strategy and attitudes.

Ultimately, the Welsh Conservatives adapted better to devolution because instead of simply accepting it, they embraced it. This progress may be prone to exaggeration and easily lost, but it marks a stark contrast with the Scottish Conservative Party. The Scottish Conservatives could not take the mental leap necessary to formulate a forward-looking strategy for their place in the Scottish Parliament. They cherished UK party links and power more than they coveted being in government in Scotland. They can only really be said to have embraced devolution with the publication of the report of the second Strathclyde Commission in 2014.

The forerunner to what eventually became the Scottish National Party was formed partly by a group of former Conservatives. Since then, the distinction between unionism and nationalism has been over-emphasised (Kidd, 2008: 264). This is the great insight of the Welsh Conservative Party. In the end, the Scottish Conservatives forgot something that the Welsh Conservatives discovered for the first time: the best unionists are nationalists.

Notes

1 Donald Dewar, for instance, was always uncomfortable with the argument that the Conservatives had 'no mandate' in Scotland (see Torrance, 2009: 189).
2 It should be noted, however, that the Scottish Conservative vote share increased slightly by 1.6 per cent at the 1992 general election.

References

Adams, J. and Somer-Topcu, Z. (2009) 'Policy Adjustment by Parties in Response to Rival Parties' Policy Shifts: Spatial Theory and the Dynamics of Party Competition in Twenty-Five Post-War Democracies', *British Journal of Political Science* 39(2): 825–846.

Adams, J., Haupt, A.B. and Stoll, H. (2009) 'What Moves Parties? The Role of Public Opinion and Global Economic Conditions in Western Europe', *Comparative Politics Studies* 42(5): 611–639.

Adams, J., Clark, M., Ezrow, L. and Glasgow, G. (2004) 'Understanding Change and Stability in Party Ideologies: Do Parties Respond to Public Opinion or Past Election Results?', *British Journal of Political Science* 34: 589–610.

Alderman, K. (2002) 'The Conservative Party Leadership Election of 2001', *Parliamentary Affairs* 55(3): 569–585.

Alonso, S. (2012) *Challenging the State: Devolution and the Battle for Partisan Credibility*. Oxford: Oxford University Press.

Arnott, M. and Macdonald, C.M.M. (2012) 'More than a Name: The Union and the Un-Doing of Scottish Conservatism in the Twentieth Century' in Torrance, D. (ed.) *Whatever Happened To Tory Scotland?* Edinburgh: Edinburgh University Press.

Ashcroft, M.A. (2005) *Smell the Coffee: A Wake-Up Call for the Conservative Party*. London: Michael A. Ashcroft.

Ashdown, P. (2001) *The Ashdown Diaries: Volume Two, 1997–1999*. London: Allen Lane.

Aughey, A. (2011) 'The Con-Lib Coalition Agenda for Scotland, Wales and Northern Ireland' in Lee, S. and Beech, M. (eds) *The Cameron-Clegg Government: Coalition Politics in an Age of Austerity*. Basingstoke: Palgrave Macmillan.

Bale, T. (2008) '"A Bit Less Bunny-Hugging and a Bit More Bunny-Boiling"? Qualifying Conservative Party Change under David Cameron', *British Politics* 3(3): 270–299.

Bale, T. (2010) *The Conservative Party: From Thatcher to Cameron*. London: Polity.

Bale, T. (2012) *The Conservatives since 1945: The Drivers of Party Change*. Oxford: Oxford University Press.

Ball, S. (2005) 'Factors in Opposition Performance: The Conservative Experience since 1867' in Ball, S. and Seldon, A. (eds) *Recovering Power: The Conservatives in Opposition since 1867*. Basingstoke: Palgrave Macmillan.

BBC News (1999) 'Richards Bailed on GBH Charge'. Accessed at http://news.bbc.co.uk/1/hi/wales/441456.stm on 9 October 2013.

BBC News (2003) 'Wiggin wants Cabinet Voice'. Accessed at http://news.bbc.co.uk/1/hi/wales/3265733.stm on 9 October 2013.

BBC News (2004) 'Richard Report and the Reaction'. Accessed at http://news.bbc.co.uk/1/hi/wales/3586389.stm on 24 July 2013.
BBC News (2005) 'Shadow Scottish Secretary Resigns'. Accessed at http://news.bbc.co.uk/1/hi/scotland/4563591.stm on 12 August 2013.
BBC News (2010a) 'National Results'. Accessed at http://news.bbc.co.uk/1/shared/election2010/results/ on 10 July 2013.
BBC News (2010b) 'David Cameron says Welsh Assembly Referendum in 2011'. Accessed at www.bbc.co.uk/news/10155091 on 18 April 2013.
BBC News (2012a) 'Scottish Independence: Cameron and Salmond Strike Referendum Deal'. Accessed at www.bbc.co.uk/news/uk-scotland-scotland-politics-19942638 on 9 June 2013.
BBC News (2012b) 'Welsh Tories Cancel Conference with Two Weeks' Notice'. Accessed at www.bbc.co.uk/news/uk-wales-politics-16631816 on 24 July 2013.
BBC News (2013) 'Ex-Tory MP Joins UKIP'. Accessed at www.bbc.co.uk/news/uk-wales-23238637 on 26 August 2013.
BBC News (2015) 'Election 2015 Results'. Accessed at www.bbc.co.uk/news/election/2015/results/Scotland on 1 July 2015.
Bille, L. (1997) 'Leadership Change and Party Change: The Case of the Danish Social Democratic Party, 1960–95', *Party Politics* 3(3): 379–390.
Bingham Centre for the Rule of Law (2015) *A Constitutional Crossroads: Ways Forward for the United Kingdom*. London: British Institute of International and Comparative Law.
Blake, R. (1985) *The Conservative Party from Peel to Thatcher*. London: Methuen.
Bogdanor, V. (2001) *Devolution in the United Kingdom*. Oxford: Oxford University Press.
Bogdanor, V. (2009) *The New British Constitution*. London: Hart Publishing.
Bohrer, R.E. and Krutz, G.S. (2005) 'The Devolved Party Systems of the United Kingdom: Sub-National Variations from the National Model', *Party Politics* 11(6): 654–673.
Boin, A. (2004) 'Lessons from Crisis Research', *International Studies Review* 6: 165–194.
Boles, N. (2010) *Which Way's Up? The Future for Coalition Britain and How to Get There*. London: Biteback.
Bolleyer, N. (2011) 'The Influence of Political Parties on Policy Coordination: A Study of Horizontal Relations in Federal Systems', *Governance* 24(3): 469–494.
Bourne, N. (2005) 'Welsh Conservatism: A Chance to Shine', St David's Lecture Speech, Welsh Governance Centre, Cardiff University, 9 March 2005.
Bradbury, J. (1997) 'Conservative Governments, Scotland and Wales: A Perspective on Territorial Management' in Bradbury, J. and Mawson, J. (eds) *British Regionalism and Devolution: The Challenges of State Reform*. London: Jessica Kingsley.
Bradbury, J. (2006) '*Territory and Power* Revisited: Theorising Territorial Politics in the United Kingdom after Devolution', *Political Studies* 54(2): 559–582.
Bradbury, J., Denver, D., Mitchell, J. and Bennie, L. (2000) 'Devolution and Party Change: Selection for the 1999 Scottish Parliament and Welsh Assembly Elections', *Journal of Legislative Studies* 6(3): 51–72.
Bratberg, Ø. (2009) 'Institutional Resilience Meets Critical Junctures: (Re)allocation of Power in Three British Parties Post-Devolution', *Publius* 40: 59–81.
Budge, I. (1994) 'A New Spatial Theory of Party Competition: Uncertainty, Ideology and Policy Equilibria Viewed Comparatively and Temporally', *British Journal of Political Science* 24: 443–467.

References

Bulpitt, J. (1982) 'Conservatism, Unionism and the Problem of Territorial Management' in Madgwick, P. and Rose, R. (eds) *The Territorial Dimension in United Kingdom Politics*. Basingstoke: Macmillan Press.

Bulpitt, J. (1983) *Territory and Power in the United Kingdom*. Manchester: Manchester University Press.

Bulpitt, J. (1986) 'The Discipline of the New Democracy: Mrs Thatcher's Domestic Statecraft', *Political Studies* 34(1): 19–39.

Burnham, P., Gilland, K., Grant, W. and Layton-Henry, Z. (2008) *Research Methods in Politics*. London: Palgrave Macmillan.

Calman Commission (2009) *Serving Scotland Better: Scotland and the United Kingdom in the 21st Century*. Accessed at www.commissiononscottishdevolution.org.uk/uploads/2009-06-12-csd-final-report-2009fbookmarked.pdf on 28 January 2013.

Cameron, D. (2009) 'Cameron: I would Govern Scots with Respect', *The Scotsman*. Accessed at www.scotsman.com/news/david-cameron-i-would-govern-scots-with-respect-1-1303858 on 12 June 2013.

Cameron, D. (2014) 'Speech on the importance of Scotland to the UK'. Accessed at www.scottishconservatives.com/2012/03/david-cameron-scottish-conservative-party-conference/.

Caramani, D. (2004) *The Nationalization of Politics*. Cambridge: Cambridge University Press.

Chhibber, P. and Kollman, K. (2004) *The Formation of National Party Systems: Federalism and Party Competition in Great Britain, India and the United States*. Princeton: Princeton University Press.

Clemens, C. (2009) 'Modernisation or Disorientation? Policy Change in Merkel's CDU', *German Politics* 18(2): 121–139.

Commission on Devolution in Wales (2011) *Empowerment and Responsibility: Financial Powers to Strengthen Wales*. Accessed at http://commissionondevolutioninwales.independent.gov.uk/files/2013/01/English-WEB-main-report1.pdf on 25 February 2013.

Conservative Party (2009) *Constitution of the Conservative Party*. London: Conservative Party.

Conservative Party (2010) *An Invitation to Join the Government of Britain*. London: Conservative Party.

ConservativeHome.com (2011) 'The Tory Masterplan to Win 36 Seats from Labour and 14 from the Liberal Democrats'. Accessed at http://conservativehome.blogs.com/majority_conservatism/2012/03/the-conservative-hq-plan-to-win-36-seats-from-labour-and-14-from-the-liberal-democrats.html on 20 June 2012.

Convery, A. (2014a) 'Devolution and the Limits of Tory Statecraft: The Conservatives in Coalition and Scotland and Wales', *Parliamentary Affairs* 67(1): 25–44.

Convery, A. (2014b) 'The 2011 Scottish Conservative Party Leadership Election: Dilemmas for Statewide Parties in Regional Contexts', *Parliamentary Affairs* 67(2): 306–327

Crickhowell, N. (1999) *Westminster, Wales and Water*. Cardiff: University of Wales Press.

Cross, W. and Blais, A. (2012) 'Who Selects the Party Leader?', *Party Politics* 18(2): 127–150.

Daily Record (2014) 'Johann Lamont Quits as Scottish Labour Leader'. Accessed at www.dailyrecord.co.uk/news/politics/johann-lamont-resigns-scottish-labour-4502765 on 25 October 2014.

Dalyell, T. (2012) *The Importance of Being Awkward*. Edinburgh: Birlinn.

Davies, A.J. (1995) *We, The Nation: The Conservative Party and the Pursuit of Power*. London: Little, Brown and Company.

Davies, R. (2002) 'Oral Evidence to Richard Commission', Richard Commission, 26 September 2002.

Della Porta, D. (2008) 'Comparative Analysis: Case-Oriented Versus Variable-Oriented Research' in Della Porta, D. and Keating, M. (eds) *Approaches and Methodologies in the Social Sciences*. Cambridge: Cambridge University Press.

Denham, A. and Dorey, P. (2005) 'A Tale of Two Speeches? The Conservative Leadership Election of 2005', *The Political Quarterly* 77(1): 35–42.

Deschouwer, K. (1992) 'The Survival of the Fittest: Measuring and Explaining Adaptation and Change of Political Parties', paper presented at the Workshop on 'Democracies and the Organization of Political Parties', European Consortium for Political Research, Limerick, Ireland, 30 March – 4 April.

Deschouwer, K. (2003) 'Political Parties in Multi-Layered Systems', *European Urban and Regional Studies* 10: 213–226.

Deschouwer, K. (2005) 'Political Parties as Multi-Level Organizations' in Katz, R.S. and Crotty, W. (eds) *Handbook of Party Politics*. London: Sage.

Detterbeck, K. (2012) *Multi-Level Party Politics in Western Europe*. Basingstoke: Palgrave Macmillan.

Detterbeck, K. and Hepburn, E. (2010) 'Party Politics in Multi-Level Systems: Party Responses to New Challenges in European Democracies' in Erk, J. and Swenden, W. (eds) *New Directions in Federalism Studies*. London: Routledge.

Douglas-Hamilton, J. (2009) *After You, Prime Minister*. London: Stacey International.

Duncan, F. (2007) 'Lately, Things Just Don't Seem the Same: External Shocks, Party Change and the Adaptation of the Dutch Christian Democrats during the "Purple Hague" 1994–8', *Party Politics* 13(1): 69–87.

Dyer, M. (2001) 'The Evolution of the Centre-Right and the State of Scottish Conservatism', *Political Studies* 49(1): 30–50.

Elias, A. (2011) 'Party Competition in Regional Elections: A Framework for Analysis'. ICPS Working Papers 295. Barcelona: Institut de Ciències Polítiques i Socials.

Elias, A. (2013) 'The Policy-Making Capacity of Political Parties in Wales' in Osmond, J. and Upton, S. (eds) *A Stable, Sustainable Settlement for Wales*. Cardiff: Institute for Welsh Affairs.

Eliassen, K.A. and Svaasand, L. (1975) 'The Formation of Mass Political Organizations: An Analytical Framework', *Scandinavian Political Studies* 10(10): 95–121.

Erk, J. and Swenden, W. (eds) (2010) *New Directions in Federalism Studies*. London: Routledge.

Evans, J. (2002) *The Future of Welsh Conservatism*. Cardiff: Institute of Welsh Affairs.

Fabre, E. (2008) 'Party Organisation in a Multi-Level System: Party Organisational Change in Spain and the UK', *Regional and Federal Studies* 18(4): 309–329.

Fabre, E. and Méndez-Lago, M (2009) 'Decentralization and Party Organizational Change: The British and Spanish Statewide Parties Compared' in Swenden, W. and Maddens, B. (eds) *Territorial Party Politics in Western Europe*. Basingstoke: Palgrave Macmillan.

Fabre, E. and Swenden, W. (2013) 'Territorial Politics and the Statewide Party', *Regional Studies* 47(3): 342–355.

Fagerholm, A. (2015) 'Why Do Parties Change Their Policy Positions? A Review', *Political Studies Review*. DOI: 10.1111/1478-9302.12078.

Fell, D. (2009) 'Lessons of Defeat: A Comparison of Taiwanese Ruling Parties' Responses to Electoral Defeat', *Asian Politics and Policy* 1(4): 660–668.

Filippov, M. Ordeshook, P.C. and Shvetsova, O. (2004) *Designing Federalism: A Theory of Self-Sustainable Federal Institutions*. Cambridge: Cambridge University Press.

Finlay, R. (2004) *Modern Scotland, 1914–2000*. London: Profile.

Finlay, R. (2012) 'Patriotism, Paternalism and Pragmatism: Scottish Toryism, Union and Empire, 1912–65', in Torrance, D. (ed.) *Whatever Happened To Tory Scotland?* Edinburgh: Edinburgh University Press.

Flinders, M. and Curry, D. (2008) 'Bi-Constitutionalism', *Parliamentary Affairs* 61(1): 99–121.

Flyvbjerg, B. (2001) *Making Social Science Matter*. New York: Cambridge University Press.

Fraser, M. (2011) 'Speech at Leadership Campaign Launch', Edinburgh, 5 September 2011. Accessed at www.murdo2011.com/campaign-launch-speech on 5 September 2011.

Gamble, A. (1993) 'Territorial Politics' in Dunleavy, P., Gamble, A., Holliday, I. and Peele, G. (eds) *Developments in British Politics 4*. London: Macmillan.

Garnett, M. (2003) 'The Leadership Gamble of William Hague' in Garnett, M. and Lynch, P. (eds) *The Conservatives in Crisis*. Manchester: Manchester University Press.

Gerring, J. (2001) *Social Science Methodology: A Criterial Framework*. New York: Cambridge University Press.

Hague, W. (1997) 'Message to Wales', *Western Mail*, September 1997.

Harmel, R. and Janda, K. (1994) 'An Integrated Theory of Party Goals and Party Change', *Journal of Theoretical Politics* 6(3): 259–287.

Harmel, R. and Tan, A.C. (2003) 'Party Actors and Party Change: Does Factional Dominance Matter?' *European Journal of Political Research* 42: 409–424.

Harmel, R., Heo, U.K., Tan, A. and Janda, K. (1995) 'Performance, Leadership, Factions and Party Change: An Empirical Analysis', *West European Politics* 18(1): 1–33.

Harris, R. (2011) *The Conservatives: A History*. London: Bantam.

Hassan, G. (2012) '"It's Only a Northern Song": The Constant Smirr of Anti-Thatcherism and Anti-Toryism' in Torrance, D. (ed.) *Whatever Happened to Tory Scotland?* Edinburgh: Edinburgh University Press.

Hayton, R. (2012) *Reconstructing Conservatism? The Conservative Party in Opposition, 1997–2010*. Manchester: Manchester University Press.

Hayton, R. and Heppell, T. (2010) 'The Quiet Man of British Politics: The Rise, Fall and Significance of Iain Duncan Smith', *Parliamentary Affairs* 63(3): 425–445.

Hazan, R.Y. and Rahat, G. (2005) 'A New Instrument for Evaluating, Comparing and Classifying Legislatures? Candidate Selection Methods', paper presented at the Workshop on Evaluating, Comparing and Classifying Legislatures, European Consortium for Political Research 33rd Joint Session of Workshops, University of Grenada, Spain.

Hazan, R.Y. and Rahat, G. (2006) 'Candidate Selection: Methods and Consequences' in Katz, R.S. and Crotty, W. (eds) *Handbook of Party Politics*. London: Sage.

Hazell, R. (2006) 'Introduction: What is the English Question?' in Hazell, R. (ed.) *The English Question*. Manchester: Manchester University Press.

Hepburn, E. (2009) 'Re-Conceptualizing Sub-State Mobilization', *Regional and Federal Studies* 19(4–5): 1–19.

HM Government (1993) *Scotland in the Union: A Partnership for Good*. Cm 2225. Edinburgh: HMSO.

HM Government (2015) *Powers for a Purpose: Towards a Lasting Devolution Settlement for Wales*. Cm 9020.

HM Treasury (2013a) *Scotland Analysis: Currency and Monetary Policy*. Accessed at www.gov.uk/government/uploads/system/uploads/attachment_data/file/191786/ScotlandAnalysis_acc-1.pdf.

HM Treasury (2013b) *Scotland Analysis: Business and Microeconomic Framework*. Accessed at www.gov.uk/government/uploads/system/uploads/attachment_data/file/209891/13-635-scotland-analysis-business-and-microeconomic-framework.pdf.

HM Treasury (2014) *Assessment of a Sterling Currency Union*. Accessed at www.gov.uk/government/uploads/system/uploads/attachment_data/file/279454/CM8815_2901849_SA_SterlingUnion_acc.pdf.

Holyrood Magazine (2011) 'Tartan Tory: The Ruth Davidson Interview'. Accessed at www.holyrood.com/articles/2011/11/14/tartan-tory-the-ruth-davidson-interview/ on 9 May 2012.

Holyrood Magazine (2015) 'Former Poll Tax Spad Given Peerage and Scotland Office Role'. Accessed at www.holyrood.com/articles/news/former-poll-tax-spad-given-peerage-and-scotland-office-role on 10 July 2015.

Hooghe, L., Marks, G. and Schakel, A.H. (2010) *The Rise of Regional Authority: A Comparative Study of 42 Democracies*. Abingdon: Routledge.

Hopkin, J. (2003) 'Political Decentralization, Electoral Change and Party Organization Adaptation: A Framework for Analysis', *European Urban and Regional Studies* 10: 227–237.

Hopkin, J. (2009) 'Party Matters: Devolution and Party Politics in Britain and Spain', *Party Politics* 15(2): 179–198.

Hough, D. and Jeffery, C. (2003) 'Multi-Level Electoral Competition: Elections and Parties in Decentralized States', *European Urban and Regional Studies* 10(3): 195–198.

Hough, D. and Jeffery, C. (eds) (2006) *Devolution and Electoral Politics*. Manchester: Manchester University Press.

Janda, K., Harmel, R., Edens, C. and Goff, P. (1995) 'Changes in Party Identity: Evidence from Party Manifestos', *Party Politics* 1(2): 171–196.

Jeffery, C. (2007) 'The Unfinished Business of Devolution: Seven Open Questions', *Public Policy and Administration* 22(1): 92–108.

Jeffery, C. and Schakel, A.H. (2013) 'Insights: Methods and Data Beyond Methodological Nationalism', *Regional Studies* 47(3): 402–404.

Johns, R., Carman, C. and Mitchell, J. (2013) 'Constitution or Competence? The SNP's Re-Election in 2011', *Political Studies* 61(1): 158–178.

Jones, J.B. (2001) 'The National Assembly Election Campaigns: Defeat in Adversity for the Conservatives', *Contemporary Wales* 14(1): 115–120.

Katz, R.S. and Mair, P. (1993) 'The Evolution of Party Organizations in Europe: The Three Faces of Party Organization', *American Review of Politics* 14: 593–617.

Katz, R.S. and Mair, P. (1994) (eds.) *How Parties Organize*. London: Sage.

Kavanagh, D. (1991) 'Why Political Science Needs History', *Political Studies* 39(2): 479–495.

Kavanagh, D. (2005) 'The Making of Thatcherism: 1974–1979', in Ball, S. and Seldon, A. (eds) *Recovering Power: The Conservatives in Opposition since 1867*. Basingstoke: Palgrave Macmillan.

Keating, M. (2009) *The Independence of Scotland*. Oxford: Oxford University Press.
Kelly, R. (2003) 'Organisational Reform and the Extra-Parliamentary Party' in Garnett, M. and Lynch, P. (eds) *The Conservatives in Crisis*. Manchester: Manchester University Press.
Kendrick, S. and McCrone, D. (1989) 'Politics in a Cold Climate: The Conservative Decline in Scotland', *Political Studies* 37(3): 589–603.
Kidd, C. (2008) *Union and Unionisms: Political Thought in Scotland, 1500–2000*. Cambridge: Cambridge University Press.
King, A. (2007) *The British Constitution*. Oxford: Oxford University Press.
Kittilson, M.C. and Scarrow, S.E. (2003) 'Political Parties and Democratization' in Cain, B.E., Dalton, R.J. and Scarrow, S.E. (eds) *Democracy Transformed? Expanding Political Opportunities in Advanced Industrial Democracies*. Oxford: Oxford University Press.
Laffin, M. and Thomas, A. (2003) 'Designing the National Assembly for Wales', *Parliamentary Affairs* 53: 557–576.
Laffin, M., Shaw, E. and Taylor, G. (2007) 'The New Sub-National Politics of the British Labour Party', *Party Politics* 13(1): 88–108.
Lang, I. (2002) *Blue Remembered Years*. London: Politico's.
Laws, D. (2010) *22 Days in May: The Birth of the Lib Dem-Conservative Coalition*. London: Biteback.
Le Duc, L. (2001) 'Democratizing Party Leadership Selection', *Party Politics* 7(3): 323–341.
Le Grand, J. (2007) *The Other Invisible Hand: Delivering Public Services Through Choice and Competition*. Princeton: Princeton University Press.
McEwen, N., Swenden, W. and Bolleyer, N. (2012) 'Intergovernmental Relations in the UK: Continuity in a Time of Change?', *British Journal of Politics and International Relations* 14: 187–343.
McKenzie, J. (2001) *Changing Education: A Sociology of Education since 1944*. Edinburgh: Pearson Education.
MacLeod, D. and Russell, M. (2006) *Grasping the Thistle*. Glendaruel: Argyll Publishing.
Mair, P. (1989) 'The Problem of Party System Change', *Journal of Theoretical Politics* 1(3): 251–276.
Major, J. (1999) *The Autobiography*. London: HarperCollins.
Meguid, B.M. (2005) 'Competition between Unequals: The Role of Mainstream Party Strategy in Niche Party Success', *American Political Science Review* 99(3): 347–359.
Meguid, B.M. (2008) *Party Competition between Unequals: Strategies and Electoral Fortunes in Western Europe*. Cambridge: Cambridge University Press.
Meguid, B.M. (2010) *Party Competition between Unequals: Strategies and Electoral Fortunes in Western Europe*. Cambridge: Cambridge University Press.
Melding, D. (2001) 'Light Blue is the Colour', speech to South Wales Central Conservatives, 21 June 2001.
Melding, D. (2009) *Will Britain Survive Beyond 2020?* Cardiff: Institute of Welsh Affairs.
Melding, D. (2012) 'Welsh Conservatism – A Lesson for Scotland?' in Torrance, D. (ed.) *Whatever Happened to Tory Scotland?* Edinburgh: Edinburgh University Press.
Melding, D. (2013) *The Reformed Union: The UK as a Federation*. Cardiff: Institute of Welsh Affairs.
Meyer, T.M. (2013) *Constraints on Party Policy Change*. Colchester: ECPR Press.
Miers, D. (2011) *Law Making in Wales: A Measure of Devolution*. Study of Parliament Group Paper No. 2. London: Study of Parliament Group.

Miller, W. (1981) *The End of British Politics? Scots and English Political Behaviour in the Seventies*. Oxford: Clarendon Press.
Mitchell, J. (1990) *Conservatives and the Union: A Study of Conservative Party Attitudes to Scotland*. Edinburgh: Edinburgh University Press.
Mitchell, J. (2003) *Governing Scotland: The Invention of Administrative Devolution*. Basingstoke: Palgrave Macmillan.
Mitchell, J. (2009) *Devolution in the UK*. Manchester: Manchester University Press.
Mitchell, J. (2010) 'The Westminster Model and the State of Unions', *Parliamentary Affairs* 63(1): 85–88.
Mitchell, J. and Bradbury, J. (2004) 'Political Recruitment and the 2003 Welsh and Scottish Elections: Candidate Selection, Positive Discrimination and Party Adaptation', *Representation* 40(4): 288–301.
Mitchell, J. and Convery, A. (2012) 'Conservative Unionism: Prisoned in Marble' in Torrance, D. (ed.) *Whatever Happened to Tory Scotland?* Edinburgh: Edinburgh University Press.
Mitchell, J. and van der Zwet, A. (2010) 'A Catenaccio Game: The 2010 Election in Scotland', *Parliamentary Affairs* 63(4): 708–725.
Morgan, K. (1999) 'Welsh Devolution: The Past and the Future' in Taylor, B. and Thomson, K. (eds) *Scotland and Wales: Nations Again?* Cardiff: University of Wales Press.
Morgan, K. and Mungham, G. (2000) *Redesigning Democracy: The Making of the Welsh Assembly*. Bridgend: Seren.
Müller, W.C. (1997) 'Inside the Black Box: A Confrontation of Party Executive Behaviour and Theories of Party Organizational Change', *Party Politics* 3(3): 293–313.
Nadler, J. (2000) *William Hague: In His Own Right*. London: Politico's.
National Assembly for Wales (2002) *Assembly Review of Procedure: Final Report*. Cardiff: National Assembly for Wales.
National Assembly for Wales (2011) *2011 Assembly Election Results*. Accessed at www.assemblywales.org/11-023.pdf on 26 August 2013.
National Assembly for Wales (2013) 'Previous Assembly Members'. Accessed at www.assemblywales.org/memhome/mem-role-response/mem-previous-members.htm on 25 July 2013.
Norris, P. and Lovenduski, J. (2004) 'Why Parties Fail to Learn', *Party Politics* 10(1): 85–104.
Norton, P. (1996) 'The Party in Perspective' in Norton, P. (ed.) *The Conservative Party*. London: Prentice Hall.
Norton, P. and Aughey, A. (1981) *Conservatives and Conservatism*. London: Temple Smith.
Osmond, J. (2007) *Crossing the Rubicon: Coalition Politics Welsh Style*. Cardiff: Institute of Welsh Affairs.
Panebianco, A. (1988) *Political Parties: Organization and Power*. Cambridge: Cambridge University Press.
Paterson, L. (2007) 'Social Democratic Education' in Keating, M. (ed.) *Scottish Social Democracy: Progressive Ideas for Public Policy*. Brussels: Peter Lang.
Rallings, C. and Thrasher, M. (2009) *British Electoral Facts*. London: Total Politics.
Ramsden, J. (1998) *An Appetite for Power*. London: HarperCollins.
Randall, N. and Seawright, D. (2012) 'Territorial Politics' in Heppell, T. and Seawright, D. (eds) *Cameron and the Conservatives: The Transition to Coalition Government*. Basingstoke: Palgrave Macmillan.

Ranney, A. (1981) 'Candidate Selection' in Butler, D., Penniman, H.R. and Ranney, A. (eds) *Democracy At The Polls*. Washington, DC: American Enterprise Institute.

Rhodes, R.A.W. (1988) *Beyond Westminster and Whitehall*. London: Routledge.

Richard Commission (2004) *Report of the Commission on the Powers and Electoral Arrangements of the National Assembly for Wales*. Accessed at http://image.guardian.co.uk/sys-files/Politics/documents/2004/03/31/richard_commission.pdf on 26 March 2013.

Richards, D. and Smith, M. (2014) 'Introduction: A Crisis in UK Institutions?' in Richards, D., Smith, M. and Hay, C., *Institutional Crisis in Twenty-First Century Britain*. Basingstoke: Palgrave.

Roberts, W. (2006) *Right from the Start: The Memoirs of Sir Wyn Roberts*. Cardiff: University of Wales Press.

Roberts, W. (2008) *Devolution in Wales: The Way Ahead – Summary Excerpt*. Accessed at www.conservatives.com/News/News_stories/2008/11/~/media/Files/Downloadable%20Files/RobertsReviewSummary.ashx on 16 March 2013.

Roller, E and Van Houten, P. (2003) 'A National Party in a Regional Party System: The PSC-PSOE in Catalonia', *Regional and Federal Studies* 13(1): 1–22.

Rose, R. (1982) *Understanding the United Kingdom*. London: Longman.

Samuels, D. (2004) 'From Socialism to Social Democracy: Party Organization and the Transformation of the Workers' Party in Brazil', *Comparative Political Studies* 37(9): 999–1024.

Sanderson Commission (2010) *Building for Scotland: Strengthening the Scottish Conservatives*. Edinburgh: Scottish Conservative and Unionist Party.

Schumacher, G., de Vries, C.E. and Vis, B. (2013) 'Why Do Parties Change Position? Party Organization and Environmental Incentives', *Journal of Politics* 75(2): 464–477.

The Scotsman (2012) 'David Cameron Tells Scotland to Copy English Reform'. Accessed at www.scotsman.com/the-scotsman/politics/david-cameron-tells-scotland-to-copy-english-reform-1-2245228 on 12 June 2012.

The Scotsman (2014) 'Tory Devo Plans "Will Fuel Yes Vote"'. Accessed at www.scotsman.com/news/politics/independence-tory-devo-plans-will-fuel-yes-vote-1-3429677 on 2 June 2014.

Scottish Conservative Central Office (2011) 'Detailed Leadership Election Results', email to the author from Scottish Conservative Central Office, 11 November 2011.

Scottish Conservative Party (1992) *The Best Future for Scotland: Scottish Conservative Manifesto, 1992*. Edinburgh: Scottish Conservative and Unionist Party.

Scottish Conservative Party (1998) *Scotland's Future: The Report of the Scottish Conservative Policy Commission*. Edinburgh: Scottish Conservative and Unionist Party.

Scottish Conservative Party (1999) *Scotland First*. Edinburgh: Scottish Conservative and Unionist Party.

Scottish Conservative Party (2003) *Time To Do Something About It*. Edinburgh: Scottish Conservative and Unionist Party.

Scottish Conservative Party (2007) *Scottish Conservative Manifesto*. Edinburgh: Scottish Conservative and Unionist Party.

Scottish Conservative Party (2011) *Common Sense for Scotland*. Edinburgh: Scottish Conservative and Unionist Party.

Scottish Conservative Party (2014) *Commission on the Future Governance of Scotland*. Edinburgh: Scottish Conservative and Unionist Party.

Scottish Labour Party (2011) 'New Position of Scottish Labour Leader'. Accessed at www.scottishlabour.org.uk/new-position-of-scottish-labour-leader on 11 December 2014.

Scottish Parliament (2011) *2011 Votes and Seats*. Accessed at www.scottish.parliament.uk/Electionresults/2011%20election/3_Votes_Seats.pdf on 28 August 2012.

Scottish Parliament (2013) 'Previous MSPs'. Accessed at www.scottish.parliament.uk/msps/24067.aspx on 1 August 2013.

Scottish Unionist Party (1949) *Scottish Control of Scottish Affairs*. Edinburgh: Scottish Unionist Association.

Seawright, D. (1999) *An Important Matter of Principle: The Decline of the Scottish Conservative and Unionist Party*. Aldershot: Ashgate.

Seawright, D. (2002) 'The Scottish Conservative and Unionist Party: "The Lesser Spotted Tory"?' in Hassan, G. and Warhurst, C. (eds) *Tomorrow's Scotland*. London: Lawrence & Wishart.

Seldon, A. and Ball, S. (eds) (1994) *Conservative Century*. Oxford: Oxford University Press.

Seldon, A. and Snowdon, A. (2005) 'The Barren Years: 1997–2005', in Ball, S. and Seldon, A. (eds) *Recovering Power: The Conservatives in Opposition Since 1867*. Basingstoke: Palgrave Macmillan.

Shipton, M. (2005) 'Assembly a Borderline Issue for Wiggin', *Western Mail*, 27 April 2005. Accessed at www.thefreelibrary.com/Assembly+a+borderline+issue+for+Wiggin.-a0131929777 on 1 March 2013.

Shipton, M. (2011) *Poor Man's Parliament: Ten Years of the Welsh Assembly*. Bridgend: Seren.

Smith, A. (2011) *Devolution and the Scottish Conservatives: Banal Activism, Electioneering and the Politics of Irrelevance*. Manchester: Manchester University Press.

Snowdon, P. (2010) *Back from the Brink: The Extraordinary Fall and Rise of the Conservative Party*. London: Harper Press.

Somer-Topcu, Z. (2009) 'Timely Decisions: The Effects of Past National Elections on Party Policy Change', *Journal of Politics* 71(1): 238–248.

Somit, A., Wildenmann, R., Boll, B. and Römmele, A. (eds) (1994) *The Victorious Incumbent: A Threat to Democracy?* Aldershot: Dartmouth.

Stewart, D. (2009) *The Path to Devolution and Change: A Political History of Scotland under Margaret Thatcher*. London: Tauris Academic Studies.

Steinmo, S. (2008) 'Historical Institutionalism' in Della Porta, D. and Keating, M. (eds) *Approaches and Methodologies in the Social Sciences*. Cambridge: Cambridge University Press.

Strathclyde Commission (1998) *Made in Scotland: The Final Report – The Way Forward for the Scottish Conservative and Unionist Party*. Edinburgh: Scottish Conservative and Unionist Party.

Swenden, W. (2010) 'Beyond UK Exceptionalism? Comparing Strategies for Territorial Management' in Stolz, K. (ed.) *Ten Years of Devolution in the United Kingdom: Snapshots at a Moving Target*. Augsburg: Wissner Verlag.

Swenden, W. and Maddens, B. (2009) 'Territorial Party Politics in Western Europe: A Framework for Analysis' in Swenden, W. and Maddens, B. (eds) *Territorial Party Politics in Western Europe*. Basingstoke: Macmillan.

Taylor, E.M. (2008) *Teddy Boy Blue*. Glasgow: Kennedy and Boyd.

Thatcher, M. (1993) *The Downing Street Years*. London: HarperCollins.
Thorlakson, L. (2009) 'Patterns of Party Integration, Influence and Autonomy in Seven Federations', *Party Politics* 15(2): 157–177.
Tilly, C. (2006) 'Why and How History Matters' in Goodin, R. and Tilly, C. (eds) *The Oxford Handbook of Contextual Political Analysis*. Oxford: Oxford University Press.
Torrance, D. (2006) *The Scottish Secretaries*. Edinburgh: Birlinn.
Torrance, D. (2009) *'We in Scotland': Thatcherism in a Cold Climate*. Edinburgh: Birlinn.
Torrance, D. (2010) *Noel Skelton and the Property-Owning Democracy*. London: Biteback.
Torrance, D. (2012) 'The Wilderness Years' in Torrance, D. (ed.) *Whatever Happened to Tory Scotland?* Edinburgh: Edinburgh University Press.
Toubeau, S. (2011) 'Regional Nationalist Parties and Constitutional Change in Parliamentary Democracies: A Framework for Analysis', *Regional and Federal Studies* 21(4–5): 427–446.
Toubeau, S. and Massetti, E. (2013) 'The Party Politics of Territorial Reform', *West European Politics* 36(2): 297–316.
Urwin, D.W. (1965) 'The Development of the Conservative Party Organisation in Scotland until 1912', *The Scottish Historical Review* 64(138): 145–162.
Urwin, D.W. (1966) 'Scottish Conservatism: A Party Organisation in Transition', *Political Studies* 44: 145–162.
Vaizey, E., Boles, N. and Gove, M. (eds) (2001) *A Blue Tomorrow: New Visions for Modern Conservatives*. London: Politico's.
Van Biezen, I. and Hopkin, J. (2006) 'Party Organization in Multi-Level Contexts' in Jeffery, C. and Hough, D. (eds) *Devolution and Electoral Politics*. Manchester: Manchester University Press.
Van Houten, P. (2009) 'Multi-Level Relations in Political Parties: A Delegation Approach', *Party Politics* 15(2): 137–156.
Verge, T. and Gómez, R. (2011) 'Factionalism in Multi-Level Contexts: When Party Organisation Becomes a Device', *Party Politics* 18(5): 667–685.
Wales Online (2007) 'Tories Trip Up over Wet Liberal Manifesto'. Accessed at www.walesonline.co.uk/news/wales-news/tories-trip-up-over-wet-2263050 on 26 July 2013.
Wales Online (2012) 'Tory AMs Chief in Call for Debate over Lack of Conservative Leader for Wales'. Accessed at www.walesonline.co.uk/news/wales-news/tory-ams-chief-call-debate-2040761 on 25 July 2013.
Walker, P. (1991) *Staying Power*. London: Bloomsbury.
Ward, J.T. (1982) *The First Century: A History of the Scottish Tory Organisation, 1882–1982*. Edinburgh: Scottish Conservative and Unionist Association.
Warner, G. (1988) *The Scottish Tory Party: A History*. London: Weidenfeld and Nicolson.
Welfare Reform Committee (2012) *Stage 1 Report on the Welfare Reform (Further Provision) (Scotland) Bill*. Accessed at www.scottish.parliament.uk/S4_Welfare_Reform_Committee/Reports/wrr-12-01w.pdf on 28 January 2013.
Welsh Conservative Party (1999) *Fair Play for All*. Cardiff: Welsh Conservative Party.
Welsh Conservative Party (2003) *Manifesto*. Cardiff: Welsh Conservative Party.
Welsh Conservative Party (2007) *Vote Welsh Conservative for a Change*. Cardiff: Welsh Conservative Party.
Welsh Conservative Party (2011) *A New Voice for Wales*. Cardiff: Welsh Conservative Party.

Wilson, F.L. (1994) 'The Sources of Party Change: The Social Democratic Parties of Britain, France, Germany, and Spain' in Lawson, K. (ed.) *How Political Parties Work from Within*. Westport: Praeger.

Wyn Jones, R. and Scully, R. (2004) 'Minor Tremor But Several Casualties: The 2003 Welsh Election' in Rallings, C., Scully, R., Tonge, J. and Webb, P. (eds) *British Parties and Elections Review 2004* 14: 191–207.

Wyn Jones, R. and Scully, R. (2012) *Wales Says Yes: Devolution and the 2011 Welsh Referendum*. Cardiff: University of Wales Press.

Index

Note: 'n.' after a page reference indicates the number of a note on that page.

All-Wales Accord 99
autonomy 17–18

Bourne, Nick 75, 84, 108, 111
brand 50–52
British Political Tradition 21

Cameron, David 28–30, 40

Davidson, Ruth 45, 48, 108
decline of Scottish Conservatives
    (1965–1999) 38–40
devolution 4–5
    evolution in Wales 80–82
    party organisational change 107
    party sub-state autonomy 108–110
    Scottish Conservatives' reaction 41–45
    Welsh Conservatives' reaction 82
dominant factions 14–15
drivers of party change 11–16
    electoral competition 15–16
    electoral defeat 15
Duncan, Peter 28
Duncan Smith, Iain 26–27

electoral competition 15–16
electoral defeat 15
    Scottish Conservatives 52–54
    Welsh Conservatives 85–87

Fraser, Murdo 48, 113, 116n.1
Fresh Future 23–24

Goldie, Annabel 48, 61, 108, 111

Hague, William 13, 23–26, 79
Heath, Edward 39
historical institutionalism 6–7
Howard, Michael 27–28, 92
Howe, Geoffrey 7

independence referendum 21, 45

leadership change 12–14, 110–112

manifestations of party change
    autonomy 17–18
    personnel 18
    policy 19
McLetchie, David 48, 61, 111

Osborne, George 21–22, 27

personnel 18
policy 19
political opportunity structure 87–88
public opinion 16

Richard Commission 80–81

Sanderson Commission 52, 59–61
Scotland Bill (2015) 45
Scotland's Future 65, 67–68
Scottish Conservative leadership election,
    2011 48–49

Scottish Unionist Party 36–37
Silk Commission 30
Smith Commission 46
statecraft 20–22
statewide parties 2–4
St David's day agreement 21
Strathclyde Commission (1998) 55–59
Strathclyde Commission (2014) 45, 71–72

Taylor, Teddy 30n.1, 73n.2
Thatcher, Margaret 1, 7, 35, 38, 56

unionism 20–21, 42, 72

Welsh nation and the Conservative Party 77–80
Welsh Office 76–77, 91
Westminster Model 21